# *Nature Norm's North Woods*

# *Nature Norm's North Woods*

## An Anecdotal Natural History

**by**

**Norman Weeks**

***Nature Norm's North Woods***

ISBN: 978-1-7953-4284-1

Copyright © 2019 Norman Weeks. All rights reserved.



Published through amazon Kindle Direct Publishing.

*Nature Norm's North Woods* is also available as a Kindle eBook.

A related book by the same author:
*Walden Contemporaneous*

## *Nature Norm's North Woods*

| | |
|---|---|
| Preface | 7 |
| Setting | 10 |
| Wildlife | 52 |
| Animal Encounters | 99 |
| Excursions | 141 |
| The Human Presence | 198 |
| Postscript | 266 |

# Preface

I was a Chicago urban boy, growing up in an environment of brick buildings, paved streets, and hard-surface alleys. Everything around me seemed inert.

What life I could find was small-scale.

My mother recognized the budding naturalist in the following exchange when I was ten years old:

"Good night, sleep tight," my mother said as she tucked me in.

"Good night," I answered.

"Sweet dreams!" my mother said.

To which I responded, "I hope I dream of bugs!"

There was that small-scale life around me, at least that, but it was not enough to satisfy a large-scale imagination. There had to be something grander elsewhere, a place wild and expansive, rich with an abundance of life.

Confined in our small apartment by winter weather, I would read Leonard Dubkin's newspaper columns on Nature in the city, that small-scale life available in my own neighborhood. Arriving home from school, I would throw aside my textbooks and delve into issues of *Outdoor Life*, *Field & Stream*, and *Sports Afield* for the faraway and the wild.

When our family could finally afford a television set, I looked forward to Thursday nights on WGN-TV, where my yearning for escape to Nature was stimulated and intensified by "Outdoors with Jim Thomas", a program of fishing, hunting, and exploration. Jim Thomas was a pioneer in real-life adventure films for television. (Later in life, I would make personal acquaintance with him through his fly-out fishing camps near Red Lake, Ontario.)

I felt a craving not only to read about and watch natural life and liveliness. Where could I experience them? On my bicycle to the green openness of Lincoln Park, along the shore of the vast Lake Michigan, a day trip necessarily. Then, school out, entire summers in the outdoors, on a farm in Batavia, Illinois owned by family friends, or to summer camps in Illinois, Indiana, and Michigan.

From Chicago, the compass of my craving seemed to be pointing North. While in the university, I took a summer job working in a resident youth camp in Wisconsin. Summer after summer, I learned and taught outdoor skills and sensitivity to children, they, like myself, come to Nature from urban confinement. I became the teaching naturalist, the program director, and finally, the camp director.

In 1970, my northwardliness went beyond Wisconsin to the utmost of United States northland, Minnesota. In Ely, I met Bob Cary, another Chicagoan gone north. Bob outfitted my first canoeing ventures into the Boundary Waters Canoe Area Wilderness. Once or twice every year thereafter, I would go on canoe trips out of Ely or from Crane Lake, outfitted there by Bob Anderson. Many years later, as camp director, I would guide teenagers from our camp on Boundary Waters excursions.

## Preface

In 1977, I happened to meet a young lady, who, in our getting acquainted, mentioned that her family owned a cabin on Pelican Lake in northeastern Minnesota. Hearing that, I immediately proposed. She laughed. But three months later, we were married--to each other and to Minnesota.

Until I retired as camp director, I was necessarily restricted to Wisconsin for woods, except for brief jaunts. Now, however, I have the full freedom of my remaining days. What better setting for many of those days than in that cabin in the Minnesota northland?

Some periods in solitude, some in marital companionship, and every day in the satisfaction of the craving and in deep, deep appreciation.

Pelican Lake, Orr, Minnesota.

# Setting

The very first time that I came to Pelican Lake, I was sure that it was a great fishing lake. I was sure even before I wet a line. I just looked out over the lake.

I saw there every kind of fish-eating bird that might be present on a northern lake: Pelican (in large numbers), eagle, osprey, loon, heron, kingfisher, cormorant, merganser, gull.

Sometimes there are so many strong indicators that you can make an inference fully confident of its certainty.

\* \* \* \* \*

The Point (*my* Point) is the northernmost of three rocky peninsulas that extend into Pelican Lake from the extreme northeast shore.

Two footpaths lead out to the tip of the Point. The one closest to my cabin begins behind my shed. It rises gradually, passes through a small grove of balsam firs, then descends at an easy slope to the bare tip of the Point. The second footpath, beyond the first, requires a steeper ascent. It rises to a high bedrock platform, upon which a neighbor has placed a handsome wood bench (little used, despite the pleasantness of its airy height and scenic view). That path then descends broad steps. The base rock there is pink granite coated with lichens and moss, with tufts of grass between the boulders, where detritus and duff serve as scant soil to root in.

*Setting*

There are a couple of shortcut paths also, one from my deck, but I do not use them. The few steps saved do not justify a back-and-forth trampling.

The peninsula out to the Point is heavily wooded, with both red pines and white pines (some lofty), balsam firs, cedars, and paper birches. Of the last, many are dead or dying, due to several recent years of drought. The pines and firs are renewing their populations, but no birch new life is to be found in the shade beneath the mature ones and elders. The deer chew off the few sprouts, I was told.

From my cabin, it's a walk of just a minute or two out to the tip of the Point and its bare thumb just above lake level.

Once there, a sweeping panorama presents itself to me, as I sit upon my observation stump. To the immediate left as I face outward is a small marshy cove; then, the peninsula of Wolff's Point, so named not from the wild canine, but from the surname of the family there; (the third peninsula, Norway Point, is blocked from view by the high rock of Wolff's Point); then, to the south, the vast expanse of the main lake with several distant islands in front of the far shore; next, to the west, a picturesque small occupied island called Hahne Island; behind that, the bare white-rock islets crowded with resting pelicans; and, last, a state forest shoreline where the sun sets behind Susan Bay.

It is a woods-and-waters scene worthy of IMAX treatment. Unlike such merely representational simulacra, the actual being-there, the feeling through all the senses, produces an experience organic, beyond the only-visual. The sterile detachedness of any electronic simulation is an experiential paltriness, a privation, compared to the full immersion of body, senses, and soul in the living natural. (Perhaps I am quaint, or eccentric, or a throwback, with such an attitude.)

– – –(Regarding immersion of body, the Point is a difficult entry and exit for swimming, due to the slippery rocks and broken boulders. I swim there, anyway, because, if you want to write about a lake, swimming is a good way to get into your subject.) – – –

During my summers living here in my cabin on Pelican Lake, the Point is my point-of contact with Nature, my vantage point, my point-of-view (not mere opinion or bias, but true seeing of reality).

\* \* \* \* \*

Pelican Lake is at its loveliest when seen from the vantage point of the Point at sunrise on a morning when the aftereffect of a cold night raises up the mists.

Tomorrow is the first of July, but the temperature this morning is 46°. When the air temperature is appreciably colder than the temperature of the water, the lake gives up some of its water as vapor.

A pale pink overlies the horizon of the far distant southern shore, but around me it is barely dawn.

From the still-dark water of the cove, the smoky white mists creep along the surface, silent ghosts. You do not see their arising out of the water. When the slight breeze gradually lifts them up, you do see their vanishing, if it can be said that you see what was there become gone. The mists that vanish are replaced by newly arisen ones in steady procession.

The mists drift across the open water, where a solitary pelican, paddling with a stately progress, is a white solidity amidst the insubstantiality of the mists.

Nearby, the form of little Hahne Island is obscured, and, beyond, the bare islets of the pelicans are completely shrouded.

From Susan Bay in the west, another wave of mists, slightly purplish, advances toward the main lake. The shoreline behind those mists cannot be seen.

The mists make the lake and landscape nebulous, water and rock and trees all become as if cloud. And I myself am in the dawn aura of a dream world.

There is an aural accompaniment to the sunrise scene: The northwoods atmospheric call of the loon, this one slightly echoed, the surprisingly loud *kronk!* of a distant frog, low grunts from the pelicans on the islets, a woodpecker's knocking, choral melodics of the little birds in the trees. The madwoman screams of passing ravens intrude a brief dissonance.

The sun still behind the trees, a 3/4s moon glows brightly overhead in a pure bluing sky.

Sunlight penetrates a gap in the trees behind the cove and forms a golden apparition upon the surface of the water.

As the sun rises over the treetops behind me, Hahne Island opposite suddenly becomes bright, even luminous. The rich green of its great pines now stands out against the dark boulder base of the island.

Beyond Hahne Island, I can now discern the white bodies crowded together on the pelicans' islets.

The advancing sunlight slowly dissipates the mists.

The scene gradually clarifies, until the pines of Hahne Island and the woods of the west shore take on a density almost jungle-like.

All around me brightens. The mists mostly gone now, save for a few wisps in the shade of the cove, dawn becomes sunny day.

Shivering a bit, I take the path back to the cabin for breakfast.

* * * * *

Henry Thoreau admitted that Walden Pond was not especially beautiful.

Compared, for example, to certain alpine lakes in the Rocky Mountains, Walden certainly lacks anything of overwhelming beauty. I've been to Walden Pond twice myself and found there little to awe my eyes. Thoreau turned Walden Pond into a beautiful symbol, anyway.

When the map of Walden Pond and the map of my own Pelican Lake are set side-by-side, the two bodies of water appear almost mirror images. The main extent of each is on the east-west axis. There are prominent bays (or, in Walden's case, coves) north and south. A cove on the west shore of Walden is reflected in the bay on the east side of Pelican.

*Setting*

As Thoreau's cabin was at the cove on the northwest shore of Walden, so my own cabin is on the northeast bay of Pelican. Like Thoreau, I hear at night the whistle of a train passing. Orr is just a long walk from my cabin, as Concord was from Thoreau's.

These correspondences of setting are not a matter of imitation or replication; they are just coincidences of topography.

There are contrasting differences, as well as correspondences, between Walden Pond and Pelican Lake.

The first is scale. Walden is a pothole of 60 acres, while Pelican Lake sprawls over 11,000 acres. The area of a body of water is a simple determinant of its impressiveness.

The old reconstructed Indian trail on the ridge along Walden enabled me to walk the circumference of the pond. Walden is circumbounded, the whole easily comprehendible. Walking around Pelican Lake—50 miles of wading mucky marshes, climbing steep bluffs, struggling through crowded undergrowth—is inconceivable.

The general outline of Walden is simple. The shoreline of Pelican Lake, by contrast, is all coves and bays, peninsulas and promontories. Then, too, the surface of Pelican Lake is broken up by over four dozen islands; Walden has no islands on it. The scenic complexity, as well as extent of area, makes Pelican Lake ungraspable to a surveying glance. As a body of water, Pelican can sustain exploratory interest in a way that Walden cannot, (except to a rare person capable of intense concentration upon the seemingly unremarkable, as Henry David Thoreau was).

Walden is unfathomable in one respect– –its great depth, believed by the gullible to be bottomless, but actually plumbed to an impressive 100+ feet. Pelican does have one hole of 35 feet, but much of it is a mere five to ten feet deep. So, at Walden, Thoreau had deep thoughts, while here at Pelican I can manage only shallow jottings.

The water of Walden Pond is clear, with little vegetation to obstruct the penetrating stare into its depths. Because it is shallow and fertile, Pelican Lake is chock full of submersed vegetation and subject to algae blooms, resulting in a general late-summer murkiness of the water.

The water of Walden is a metaphor for Thoreau's writing, deep and clear. I hope my own writing is a contrast, not a correspondence, to the water of Pelican Lake.

\* \* \* \* \*

When the sun is low in the west, glistening on the surface of Pelican Lake, it projects the pattern of the waves on the water through the window and a sliding glass door between rooms onto a far wall in my cabin. The wall becomes a screen displaying a moving image, the windblown waves undulating.

. . . And now the window next to the wall mirrors Pelican Lake itself in a mirage of vivid reality.

I am "at the lake", but now the lake has come inside with me. Except that it left its water behind.

That lake in the window. . . Or is it behind the window? The real lake is behind me, I know. What is that other one in front of me? Image? Imagination?

I know that I am on a peninsula. Might I actually be on an island? Aren't we all islanders?

* * * * *

The full moon raises his head above the tree line on one shore just as the sun lowers his head below the tree line of the facing shore....

Astronomical peekaboo!

* * * * *

If you like to have your feet on solid ground, northern Minnesota is the place for you.

This is the land of rock. Not pebbles and stones here and there, but big slab rock under everything, boulder piles and jumbles scattered atop the base rock, rock faces, rock slopes, rock heights. A hike here is rock-climbing, a descent to a lake shoreline is a clambering over boulders. The trees grow out of crevices in rock, and all the animals--nothing soft to dig through--must find their shelter between, beneath, and among the rocks. If a human erects a house here, he can be sure of a solid foundation. He can be sure,--he can take it for granite.

No earthquake would attempt to disturb these rocks, for they have been here over 2-1/2 billion years, and they intend to stay put. The glaciers have rearranged some of them, but that was just a scouring

*Setting*

of the surface. This land is solid deep down, a *terra* very *firma*.

When we used to take camping trips into the Boundary Waters, our outfitter would provide us with roll-up foam pads for under our sleeping bags. A futile provision that was. Our main mattress was rock. Our only hope was to try to find a slight concave contour surface that might complement our body's convex form.

Nor is this terrain on the level. Setting up the camp stove could be exasperating. My partner would place the stove on a flat rock, from which the stove would slowly slide off. He then found a ledge for the stove and put on a pot, which pot began its slide. He turned the stove this way and that, around the 360° of the compass, and finally cried out, "There's not a level spot in this whole damn country!"

He was right, for which blame the glaciers.

We *voyageur* fishermen also faced the dangers of the *slippery rock trick*. (The *trick* was such a one as might be performed by a clumsy acrobat, i.e., falling down while flailing arms and legs.) Fishing from shore, which, of course, was all rock, we had to beware of a wet rock made slippery by moss and slime. More than once one of us had the slope slip out from under and the bones crash to hard impact upon the rock below.

Yesterday, here on Pelican Lake, I heard a motorboat engine come to a sudden crashing halt, and the driver burst forth with foul language. Many rocks are marked on the lake maps and hazard markers have been put out, but, with low water, newly emerged rocks rudely intrude themselves upon motorboats. We canoeists are smug in our immunity from high-speed violent collisions with rocks.

The rocks and boulders are inert, but they are not sterile. Lichens and mosses find them a suitable enough bed. Lichens, I have read, secrete an acid that etches into the rock's surface to gain a secure hold. Maybe through the aeons to come it will be lichens' acid that pulverizes all the rocks of northern Minnesota.

Just a far-future fantasy, that.

The freeze-thaw cycle of ice does crack the rock. Canoeing along a shoreline, you may see a boulder big as a house neatly cleaved in two by the ice. The rain beats down, the waves smack the boulders on the shoreline, tree roots pry rocks apart. Such various processes of erosion and breaking-up are going on.

And yet, the 2-1/2 billion-year-old rock is still here. It is the geology under all the biology, the lifeless upon which, among which, all life lives.

\* \* \* \* \*

Edgar A. Guest once wrote a piece of verse, the opening line of which was, "It takes a heap o' livin' in a house t' make it home."

Up here there's a town called Northome. It's hard to find that second syllable in the first.

The northland is forbidding to one seeking a setting for an easy way of life. It takes a heap o' livin' to find in it a congenial environment.

*Setting*

Someone in our neighboring state, North Dakota, proposed deleting the word *North* from the state's name to make the place sound less awful. Our neighboring Minnesota county, Koochiching, has even resorted to offering free land to anyone with a trade or profession who would move to the county.

The first deterrent presented by the northland is, of course, the cold. Not only the winters– –"The coldest spot in the country today is International Falls, Minnesota, with a bone-chilling –32°," warns the weatherman on a TV station in the South– –, but also the other three seasons. Some summers never warm up enough to merit the name; 2009 was a recent one I shivered through. Winters are dark and frigid, springs and autumns chilly, summers thermally deficient, to the frustration of vacationers.

Then there are the bugs. Mosquitoes, spiders, wasps, hornets, bees, wood ticks, deer ticks, blackflies, deerflies, horseflies, flies that look like innocent house flies but attack a canoeist's ankles, gnats, and biting midges (*no-se-ums*). Tiny afflictions, true, but sometimes bloodsuckingly relentless.

Trees and lakes are pretty, but, as I said, this is basically a land of rock. How can you make a comfy home on a hard rock pile?

Back to more harsh weather: The gale winds and storms and blizzards drive you out of the open, reducing you to the level of the local animals, desperately looking for any shelter hole to crawl into. What's the good of a picturesque outdoors, if you're frequently driven from it?

I first came to northern Minnesota forty years ago on a fishing expedition with fellows from my old Chicago neighborhood. The Boundary Waters advertised fabulous fishing, and it did not disappoint in that regard. As for the northland rigors, my partners, soft urbanites that they were, considered those suffering that had to be endured for the sake of the fishing. If they could have caught the same fish in their own backyard ponds —(so they may have imagined)—, they would have stayed at home, on an easy chair, beer in hand, fishing rod extended out the window.

Through subsequent Boundary Waters trips—seventeen as I have recently counted—, my partners were still just discomforted fishermen suffering the weather, the bugs, the rocks on a chaotic landscape, plus the irksome labors of paddling, portaging, camp set-up, and cooking. (Wanting to say something positive, one of them remarked, "This is a nice country...if you like the color green.")

Like my companions, I fished fanatically, but I gradually came to acquire a wider perspective. The fewer trip mates I had, the better I could relate to the northland environment, until, when I went solo, I related directly, without dissonance or distraction.

I found myself quite taken with the north woods, not at first as a prospective home, but as an exotic adventure destination with many natural attractions. I took the rigors as bracing challenges.

Most people come here temporarily, for recreational purposes. Some of that recreation is exploitive and extractive,—catching fish, shooting animals, or at least picking wild fruits and wildflowers. The dozen resorts and lodges on Pelican Lake cater to that exploitive recreation.

*Setting*

There are also seasonal residents, those who can take just so much of this environment, then they're out of here, back to their home; I myself am just a seasonal. (However, because I am here only during summer, I'm able to produce this literary rarity, a completely ice-free, snow-free Minnesota book.) Winter hardship holds no allure for me. Ice fishing is more ice than fishing.

The local people—200+ in the town of Orr—have the northland as their year-round domicile. Besides the harshness of their environment, their living is made further difficult by the effort to make a living. Outside of logging and mining —(exploitive livelihoods)—, the trades, odd jobs, and fishing tourism, there is little in the way of employment here. I met one local who scrapes by on three jobs, one of which is in the grocery store, the others as custodian of two waste transfer stations. In the meager area economy, he covers both input and output.

After several summers of rehabilitative work on my cabin, I have a house in the woods that feels like a home, is homey. Electric lights, stove, refrigerator, sinks, flush toilet, shower, rocking chair, bed with cushy mattress,—all the requisites of domestic comfort. (Well, my little electric heater is sometimes inadequate.)

And when I step outside, it is not into a fearsome and forbidding landscape. I now feel a homeyness there too, one slowly developed through days and years, that heap o' livin', of gradual familiarizing. I have settled in to the setting.

Today the great blue heron is in his usual spot, just where he belongs. Me too. At home here.

\* \* \* \* \*

I drew a wine glass from the cupboard, went out the door, and headed to the very tip of the Point.

Arriving there, I knelt down on two knees. Leaning forward, I braced myself with a straight right arm, the spread fingers of my hand a support upon the rock.

As I extended my left arm out over the water, a floating swarm of whirligig beetles whirligigged away from me.

I dipped the wine glass into Pelican Lake, a water strider skittering away to escape being scooped into the glass.

I stood up and held the full glass of Pelican Lake water in the bright light of the sun.

Suspended throughout the glass were the green spheres of algae. Tiny creatures flinched and flitted about. A glassful of life.

There is life in the water, water itself the very medium of life, our sustenance, even main component of our own organic human bodies.

The north woods provides abundance of life-giving water in the innumerable lakes. No one here need go thirsty.

Yet, although I held the water in a wine glass, I was not going to drink it. The menagerie of microlife in Pelican Lake water might include *giardia*, an intestinal parasite sometimes spread into surface water by deer, beavers, and birds.

*Setting*

A Native American woman I once hired to guide me on a hike in the Rocky Mountains of Montana told me that she used to dip her cup into the fresh-flowing cold streams, until, just after a deep drink, she happened to walk upstream, where she came upon the putrid stinking carcass of an elk sprawled in the middle of the stream.

Microbes likely to cause intestinal distress are most common in shallow water and in the surface layer of lakes, so, on wilderness excursions, I never drew drinking water from the shoreline by my campsite or from any shallows.

When I was in my canoe out in the middle of one of the huge deep lakes of the Boundary Waters, however, I felt no reluctance to satisfy thirst by dipping my tin cup over the side. I always found the northern lake water wholesome and salubrious.

If in doubt about drinking water in the wild, you can always subject it to a chemical disinfectant; that will make it safe, if repugnant to taste. Or you can do what I did when I lived in rural Brazil, that is, boil the water to sterility.

Chemicals distasteful and cooking fuel a resource to be rationed when camping in the wild, there is an alternate technique for obtaining good potable water, as follows: Tie a long nylon cord to the finger hold of a gallon glass jug. In a mesh bag place a stone of sufficient weight to sink the empty jug and tie the mesh bag to the cord near the jug. Whittle a stopper to replace the jug's cap. Bore a fine hole through the stopper top to bottom, insert a string of the same length as the nylon cord through the stopper from the top, and knot it at the bottom. Stopper the jug tightly. Paddle out to the deepest part of a large lake and slowly lower the jug down into the cold clear depths. Pull out the stopper, let the jug fill up, and draw up your gallon of drinking water.

You're getting the best of the local water that way. (I am reporting my experiences here, not recommending anything. I disclaim all liability. Still, the one and only time I contracted *giardia* was from a well in a suburban Chicago forest preserve,—water supposedly tested and certified. The amoebic dysentery I suffered in Brazil was not from my boiled water, but, likely, from a contaminated meal served to me.)

I do not drink the water of Pelican Lake. I have no well to supply my cabin, either. I pump water from the lake for washing and bathing. Pelican Lake being so shallow, I cannot employ the deep-water jug technique, so, while resident in my cabin, I have to resort to bottled water, an elixir from sources, the labels claim, of glacial purity and exquisite taste.

I poured the wine glass of water back into its mix of life in Pelican Lake....

Walking back to my cabin, I began to think about another elemental of the physical environment, namely, soil.

The peninsula to the Point is mostly bedrock. I might find a mat of soft, plush moss, but, if I lift that up, there would be rock again.

The peninsula is littered with the trunks, limbs, branches, and twigs of fallen trees. Nature is a worse litterer than any camper, but Nature's litter is organic and recyclable into new life.

The vegetal litter on the peninsula is in various states of decay. The bacteria, fungi, and miscellaneous microorganisms whose work it is to recycle organic material are necessarily slow workers in the northland, because frigid winters and generally cool temperatures throughout the year retard their labors. So different from the tropical rainforest of my familiar Amazon, where constant warmth and moisture conduce to such speedy and efficient recycling that most of the nutrients there are in the living trees, very little left available as resource in the ground.

The topsoil on the Illinois farm where I spent my boyhood summers was 14" of rich, dark black humus. Nothing like that in glacier scraped and scoured northern Minnesota. Past glacial history and present climate conspire against soil formation here. Even the tough little conifer needles are obstinately resistant to recycling processes.

Instead of soil—by which I mean good black dirt—, what I find under the litter is mostly that detritus and duff I mentioned before. Detritus is disintegrated particles of the ubiquitous rock. Duff is the very incompletely decayed organic matter.

Down on my knees again, I drew my bare hand along the ground. The heel of my hand scraped bedrock.

Now, in examining the microlife of water or soil-such-as-it-is, I might resort to a magnifying glass or a microscope. I have the former in my cabin, as binoculars too, but I don't find myself using either very much.

Man is the tool-making and tool-using animal. We have developed all sorts of instruments for scientific investigation. The biologist takes an instrumental approach to Nature, uses instrumental means to knowledge.

Unlike the biologist, a naturalist considers knowledge not the goal, but only a means. The goal of the naturalist is contact, relatedness, and, ultimately, attunement. To strive for that goal, the naturalist uses simple sense perception, without instrumental intermediary. Instruments may detach and obstruct, rather than further, the naturalist's striving. Nature is not to be objectified, for how can we objectify the Great Process of which we ourselves are a part?

Some biologists may become naturalists, but few naturalists are inclined the other way. In our contemporary world, science expands, as Nature diminishes. The naturalist has become an antiquarian, on the way to becoming an obsolete type.

\* \* \* \* \*

I once remarked to a *voyageur* partner of mine that, when you see the far-off shoreline from a canoe, the woods seem all alive, but when you approach and then land, you see that half the trees are down and dead.

The actual is not revealed by just one perspective; sight is not insight. You have to look from far and near, today and again tomorrow, by day and by night, under sun, under rain, under the moon, in all conditions and through all the seasons over years. A stand of trees appears static, but it is a complex of dynamic processes.

*Setting*

The trees that are down and dead are undergoing a slow recycling of their materials into nutrients for those trees still alive. Some standing trees, although alive now, may be diseased and dying, soon to fall and add their bulks to the compost heap. The vigorous living trees race one another upwards toward the sun; the losers in that competition will join the dying and the dead. The mature living trees produce their seeds and cones for the next generation, but it may be shade-tolerant sprouts of a different species that will compose and dominate the forest to come.

The reality of the forest is not in the static view, the stand; it is in the dynamic processes,—coming-to-life, emergence, growth, competition, reproduction, flourishing, decline, death, decay, recycling, succession, and renewal.

These woods of northeastern Minnesota are not the *forest primeval*, as I am reminded by every logging truck that passes up and down Highway 53. Most of the trees are second-growth or third-growth, any untouched groves of centuries-old pines few and isolated, compared to a former presence that might be considered the aboriginal forest. What has grown back after the logging may not be what was there before; in any case, regrowth at first is done by the fast-growing scrawny, like aspens and birches. So-called reforestation, a planting of rows of a single species, raises a new stand as monotonous as an Iowa cornfield, and life-poor besides.

Winds may lay low sections of forest, insects or disease pathogens may ravage certain tree species, weather takes its toll, and long-term climate change may doom some kinds of trees and prove a boon to others. Some of these various processes of change in the forest are unperceived, even when they may prove inevitable. "You can't see the forest for the trees" is necessarily true.

My cabin is surrounded by the *boreal forest*, the north woods, spires and steeples of conifer—spruce, fir, pine—, along with birches, aspens, some maples, and assorted other trees that can steel themselves against the severe winters,—the winters not so severe as they used to be, which will bring about future changes in the arboreal composition of the forest where I spend my current days.

As these trees live upon the rocks, so a variety of local life-forms lives upon and among the trees. Lichens and mosses attach to trunk, limb, and branch, microorganisms dwell among the roots, insects burrow through bark and feed off leaves, birds snatch up those insects and set up an avian nursery in or on the tree, squirrels sustain themselves on seeds and cones, hawks enjoy a squirrel dinner. An entire pyramidal community of creatures has its existential base upon the forest ecosystem.

You can look into the woods but not see through. You can walk into the woods but not penetrate. A boreal forest is not a topography that is easily passable, like an urban park with its conveniently spaced trees and an open, level mowed lawn. A forest throws up obstacles to passage,—downed dead trees, clumps of tightly packed saplings, limbs and branches strewn across the ground. Here in northern Minnesota, the forest also presents hills, slopes, boulders and bogs, thickets and dense brush. Pathless passage is laborious.

In mid-summer a dense forest sometimes seems all woven together by spider webs; you get all sticky with their strands.

*Setting*

Native Americans, the original *voyageurs*, and explorers all traveled water routes, entering the woods only to blaze portages between bodies of water. Camps and communities were riverside or lakeside.

Native Americans hunted the forest, of course, but the deep woods is not so abundant of life as is, for example, the Great Plains. The stereotypical woods animal, the white-tailed deer, was nowhere so abundant in the virgin forest as it has since become on land cleared for fields, pasture, and suburban green spaces.

The deep woods can seem silent and lifeless. It is along the forest edges, by open land or, better, by a body of water, that there is quantity and rich variety of life. The most productive place for a naturalist, therefore, is a cabin on some shore, like my own on Pelican Lake.

\* \* \* \* \*

Across the expanse of the northern horizon over the lake I see a grayish haze. The north wind carries the faint smell of wood smoke. Forest fires.

The north woods of Ontario is ablaze. Yesterday, I read in the newspaper that more than 2,300 square miles of forest have burned in the province this year, and several thousand firefighters, drawn from the Canadian provinces and from the United States Great Lakes states, are now engaged in attempting to beat back the many outbreaks.

Campers careless with their fires are sometimes implicated in torching the forest. I remember that, as a boy, I was told by Smokey the Bear that only I could prevent forest fires. How that could be true about a boy sitting in a Chicago apartment many miles from any woods had me puzzled. When, as an adult, I took to the north woods, I was always scrupulous about my fire-building. I cleared the area around the fire pit, kept my fire small and controlled, and drenched the coals before I left. I would play my part in preventing forest fires.

Campers are occasional culprits responsible for accidents of forest fire, true, but it is lightning that is the arsonist.

Many thunderstorms break out through the northwoods summer. If the thousands and thousands of lightning-to-ground strikes are not accompanied by enough rain to douse wood set aflame, the forest begins to burn. Driving winds may then turn the landscape into inferno.

The scene of a raging forest fire is the image of hell and holocaust. What other natural phenomenon could be more destructive to all forms of life in the woodlands?

Forest fire seems annihilative. And yet...

There are surface fires and crown fires. The former may just smolder along, burning off forest floor debris and shrubs, or, if more intense, may scorch the trunks of living trees. Crown fires, impelled by high winds, set the canopy aflame and will kill off the over-story.

Trees are killed in any forest fire, but the forest itself will not be killed off. It will come back.

As there has always been lightning, so there have always been lightning-caused forest fires. The forest endures because of defenses and adaptations of the trees. Pines have a thick bark resistant to fire, jack pine cones are actually opened by fire, birches can resprout from roots, aspens from suckers. The birds, squirrels, and the winds carry in seeds from unburned areas. After fire, the forest will come back.

As a natural process, lightning-ignited fire effects a decomposition of organic materials and a recycling of locked-up nutrients back into the forest system. It is not the catastrophe one would conclude from the image of the blazing inferno.

For eighty years of the twentieth century, the forest service agencies, seeing only the destructive aspect of forest fires, followed a policy of vigorous firefighting, attempting to stamp out any flare-up. The goal was a totally fire-free forest.

The consequence of that policy was a forest become senescent, filled with old, diseased, decrepit, dying trees and a forest floor piled up with dead material, all the more fuel for any fire. Such conditions produced fires—like those now afflicting Ontario—so rampant as to overmaster attempts at suppression.

By 1987, the constructive role of forest fires was understood and the policy changed. Now, not only are some lightning-caused fires permitted to burn (if not threatening to human interests), but the forest service itself conducts *prescribed burns* to promote regeneration of young healthy forests and the various birds and animals that can thrive in them. Smokey the Bear has taken up the torch.

*Setting*

"Forest fires were as vital as rain, snow, wind, and temperature in shaping the ecosystem." So wrote Miron Heinselman in *The Boundary Waters Wilderness Ecosystem,* the masterwork in the understanding of northern forest ecology. Fire can be considered a kind of weather.

It may seem paradoxical, even perverse, to welcome the destruction of the forest we are looking at for the sake of a forest to come. Yet, the static leads to death. Fire is an essential dynamic of the living forest.

\* \* \* \* \*

The winds were ripping all day today.

The tops of the birches and aspens were being whipped about like prairie grasses. The pines and cedars put up their characteristic stiff-fiber resistance; even so, some of the medium-size pines swayed the whole length of their trunks, slightly, forward and back.

As I mentioned earlier, after several years of drought in northern Minnesota, many birches have died and are now likely to be toppled by the winds. I saw one dead birch fallen against a utility pole, another atop a boathouse. One spindly deceased birch angles over my own cabin. I'll have to take it down before it slices toward my bed to my rude awakening.

This northern Minnesota ground, all rock and more rock, has scant topsoil, let alone penetrable earth. Consequently, the trees, groping their toes around the boulders, often fail of a foothold. The winds roar and some trees fall entire, the exposed cluster of roots sometimes still grasping boulders in their tentacles. Just outside my cabin door, a 14-foot balsam fir, all green and vibrant, got hard pushed against an underlying boulder by the winds and so broke off at the base.

Pelican Lake was in a froth of whitecaps today, the accompaniment to summer rainstorms surging through. We expect the wind with the rain. Here in the northland, on blue-sky days too you may be browbeaten, by fair-weather gales. When a sudden gale springs up on a canoeist in the middle of a large lake or open bay, raising whitecaps, a tame activity may become dangerous.

Or at least frustrating. Once, on a canoe trip in the Boundary Waters, my partner and I could make no progress against the headwinds, despite my partner's muscularity applied with zeal to the paddling and my own skillful steering. It was the end of our trip, but we knew that we would not be able to make it to the pickup point. Our outfitter anticipated that, for, with motorboat a match for wind and waves, he, knowing our return route, followed it until he rescued two windbound *voyageurs* stranded helpless on a rock pile.

Northland gales are the bane of the canoeist. You would think that, by chance, the winds might sometimes come from behind you, thereby speeding you on your course. Yet, when I have had paddle in hand, I always seem to have had the wind in my face. I'm hard-put to remember a single tailwind....

Well, there must have been some.

I was in a group of canoeists once, when one participant got the idea to lash a tarp between two paddles, which, held aloft, would act as a sail and propel the canoe without effort. The stern man was to

*Setting*

use the spare paddle as a rudder. The rig seemed to work at first, but then the wind shifted contrary, blew the paddles down, and collapsed the sail.

Expanding the idea, someone else suggested using two paddles lashed to thwarts to make a catamaran out of two canoes, then each canoe to be outfitted with the makeshift sail, and so, lashed together for stability and double-sailed, the craft would skim swiftly across the water of the big bay. Ingenious, but perhaps just childishly naive.

The wind strong enough to propel a sail-rigged loaded double canoe but capricious and contrary once again, the whole nautical contrivance threatened to fall apart into flotsam. All the paddles now occupied in the lashings, there were none available to control or advance. The whole idea was dashed by the winds.

At the same time that I was on a canoe/camping excursion in the Boundary Waters, July 4, 1999, there occurred a *derecho*, a straight-line windstorm, northeast of Ely, Minnesota. That wind knocked down from 10% to 100% of the trees in a swath 4 to 12 miles wide by 30 miles long, over 350,000 acres of blowdown, a major wind disaster, if not upon human communities, none of which was in the path. Nature too suffers catastrophes, although she files no insurance claims.

Tent stakes, like tree roots, often fail to fasten secure among the underlying boulders. I was gathering firewood around the campsite once, when a mini-*derecho* puffed up my tent, plucked it into the air, and drove it down a hillside like a deflating blimp. Throwing aside the firewood bundle, I dashed after my tent, scrambled down the hillside, and managed to leap upon

*Setting*

the tent, using my body weight to stop it from blowing into the lake.

There are no hurricanes in the northland, but, even so, the wind is a fearsome force here. It shakes and breaks the trees, arouses fright and frustration in canoeist or camper.

* * * * *

Today is chilly, rainy, and blustery.

The guests at the resort get in the boats and venture out on the lake, anyway. They have only a few precious days of vacation and want to get their money's worth.

We residents can wait it out. This is the kind of day when the outdoorsman becomes an indoorsman. A naturalist turns domestic, puttering around in his cabin.

A day for lying around on the couch and browsing through field guides.

Under these hostile conditions, Nature is better experienced through a window.

Even though I am resident here during the good weather season, that doesn't mean that there will be actual good weather.

Northern Minnesota is a place where you enjoy steaming chicken noodle soup in the middle of July.

* * * * *

Sitting on my observation stump on the tip of the Point, Pelican Lake spread out before me, on a long early summer evening.

To the south, the sky is a soft blue, paled by the sun's gradual recession. There is a low long line of static cumulus clouds, bright white in reflection, their bottoms flat. The view to the south presents a picture of stability and calm.

But in the west, dark gray menacing masses of clouds are "Uh-oh!" ominous. Gathering themselves, mounting higher, bulking up, those clouds are in an advance to storm.

The contrast between what the south shows and what is now apparently coming toward me is like two different places or two different days at the same place, yet it is over one Pelican Lake on one summer evening time.

Assessing the full surround of the weather situation, I rotate my gaze from that tranquil south to the east and north, where some of the threat has passed by, to the west, where I stare hard at what's coming.

In the far west, I detect the faint slanted vertical path of gray, which means hard rain.

The dark cloud masses press their approach, as I sit exposed.

Now I am directly under the full darkness and menace, a cloak about to envelop and smother me. I feel the thrill of danger, the change in atmospheric pressure causing a change in my blood pressure.

A cold forewind to the rain now ruffles the waters of Pelican Lake, chills me. The blast is at the same time frightening and refreshing. I have seen no lightning, heard no thunder. I will stay put.

The squall I observed in the far distance now rushes in. From the shore where the pelicans hunch on their bare rocks, the squall pounds across Pelican Lake.

The rain drives down, the chill winds push along the waves in driving pulses.

Two motorboats, whose occupants were oblivious to the imminence of the squall, make a mad dash to land. One heads to Wolff's Point; a man and a woman, both already drenched, stumble onto the dock in the full downwind subjection to the squall.

I get up from the stump and back upwind into the shelter of the woods on the peninsula. Just some few drops of the downpour penetrate my cover and spot my head and jacket.

. . . I came in to write this, then, having finished, I leave the cabin and walk out to the Point again.

The stump is now wet to sit upon, so I stand looking around at the aftermath.

To the south, the sky is paler now, that long line of static clouds still extending across the lake as before. Seeming continuity of stability.

To the west, some of the sun's fading gold penetrates or overrides the scattered remnants of the squall clouds.

*Setting*

A chill but slight afterwind blows, just enough to lap the shore boulders with liquid licking.

To the east, I see the dark of the squall fully passed and receding toward the treetop skyline.

The swallows have resumed their dinnertime aerial insect dining....

A squall, just a passing event. Not to be fled from, like our oblivious and frustrated motorboaters made miserable by interruption, or missed completely, like those sitting inside staring at the stupefying glow of the TV screen at the time. A natural event to be experienced, to be felt in the flesh, the full fright and awe of it. The spectacle, the awareness of vulnerability, and even the wet skin when it is all over.

\* \* \* \* \*

I feel limitations on my experiential understanding and my appreciation of the northland.

My first limitation is time. A summer seasonal, I am not here to witness the awakening of early spring, the gradual shutdown of autumn, or the silent depths of extreme winter. I experience and observe just some few stages of the total northland seasonal processes.

As a restriction of time, so a narrowness of perspective.

I have selected the Point as the basic locus of my contact with, and relatedness to, this northland environment. I'm on solid ground there; that's a good start. And the view before me is panoramic. From a strong base the wide view,—that is the conducive situation of the Point.

Even with such advantageous positioning, there are limitations. At the Point, I am, as it were, out on a limb, in reference to the unseeable depths of the woods behind me. Also, my view of Pelican Lake is a surface view only.

What if I shed my clothes and step off the Point into Pelican Lake? Down into the water, aswim. The water is cold, uncongenial to my warm body. The strands of weeds try to entangle my legs; I stub my toe upon a submerged boulder. If backing away from the Point, I have to tread water, exerting myself physically, not calm and still as an observer should be. I've got to struggle to keep my head above water. What I can see while swimming is only what a frog sees. From the surface, I look upwards and forwards, but still see nothing of the depths.

To experience the lake better, I might go out upon it in my canoe. Afloat in the very center of the lake. In my canoe I stay comfortably dry, the body of the canoe between my body and the liquid reality of the lake. Back on the Point, my sweep of view was just a bit more than 180°; in my canoe, I can take in the full 360°. It's a roundabout view, once again of the surface; my looking down does not penetrate the murky water. As for the woods, I see only the trees fronting the shoreline, nothing behind. At least the dome of the heavens is wide open to the view from my canoe. All I can see there is infinite emptiness.

I want to get to know the woods, so I hike into them, well away from any trail or path. The full of the solid continent, not just the slim appendage of the

Point, is beneath my feet now. The trees around me rise like cluttered columns in a cathedral, thrown-up obstacles to my searching view. Their high canopies also block out the heavens and the sun. I've come into the woods to see something, only to be thrown into the dark. Not the dark of night, certainly, but a dim obstructed view, nonetheless.

In this northern Minnesota terrain, I can climb a hill and step out to the edge of a high bluff overlooking lake or woods. A thrilling view, but is it a revelatory one? Maybe I become lightheaded up there, too dizzy to see straight. Anyway, farsightedness is an optical infirmity.

For an even more altitudinal view, I can board a floatplane, as I have done many times. Floatplanes cruise just above the treetops, not like a jet in its stratospheric remoteness. The Nature of earth, woods, and waters passes by just under me, as I press my face to the window of the plane. The plane is moving, but it's as if the plane is still, while the earth rotates under my gaze. Everything passes too quickly for assimilation. I get glimpses only. What am I overlooking while I am over looking?

The floatplane skims the water in its landing, the woods in front of me again, not beneath me, I now on the lake, not over it. Back down into Nature, I think. I disembark on the dock.

A short while later, I'm back where I started from, on the Point, staring out. Have I experienced anything of the essence?

Demoralized, I retreat into my cabin. Nature is on the outside now. Any view from a cabin window is necessarily confined by the window frame and insulated by the glass.

I seem to have exhausted all the possible perspectives upon the northland and found each in some ways unsatisfactory.

The limitation of any chosen viewpoint is not only the external circumstances it presents; there are also inadequacies of awareness and receptivity the human carries along everywhere and anywhere. Seeing, entering into, and becoming part of, Nature,—the attainment of attunement,—is frustrated by ourselves, not just by the otherness of the environment. Even if we could be omnipresent, we would still see so little and miss so much.

One perspective remains: I look at Nature with my mind's observational eye. The mind's eye is a reflective mirror. It holds a mirror to a mirror, for the Nature out there is also the nature within. Perhaps sight may become insight yet.

This book is my perspective, a literary one. No different from all the other possible views, it too suffers its limitations. What is here is not Nature; it is only a limited report of what my eyes—and my mind's eye—have seen.

\* \* \* \* \*

July 4, 2012.

At two o'clock I lay down for an afternoon nap. I dozed off.

When I awoke, it was unexpectedly dark. What, had I slept into the arrival of evening?

*Setting*

I looked at my watch. 2:15.

An uneasy feeling came over me.

I got up, went outside, and looked around.

I decided to take the path to the Point, from which I could look out over the lake to see what might be coming.

Once there, I sat down on the observation stump.

To the southwest I saw a dark, thick curtain wall of ominous portent. In front of that was a leaden roll of gray cloud.

Suddenly, the south shoreline of Pelican Lake disappeared utterly. The line of storm pushed across the lake's expanse at a swiftness I had never seen before. The leaden roll of the forefront cloud took on a slight tornadic rotation.

Alarmed, I leapt up, instantly changing from spectator to refugee. I dashed back down the path as fast as my body could run.

The wind came over just as I got inside the cabin.

Sited as it is on a slab of bedrock, my cabin has no basement for secure shelter. I took a position at the front door, which was the part of the cabin most downwind of the blow.

Despite the tornadic rotation I had spotted in the forefront cloud, this was a straight line high wind. A *derecho*! The tops of the trees were hard pushed by the surge of wind.

*Setting*

There was no loud roar. What I heard was the creaking and cracking of tree limbs and the thudding of broken branches upon the cabin roof above me.

The wind surge (which I would later find out was clocked at 90 miles per hour) was accompanied by a few intermittent short downbursts of rain.

As I stood within the door frame, looking through the glass panel of the storm door, apprehensive and a bit frightened, a birch in front of me broke off three feet from its base and sliced down to earth parallel to my car and just a foot from it.

What if I were in a tent in this, I wondered? I hoped that my cabin would prove protective enough. . .

In about twenty minutes the *derecho* was over.

Before stepping outside, I checked the thermometer. The temperature had dropped 18° during the event.

Myself safe and sound, I then ventured out to assess the environmental damage.

A felled balsam lay upon my cabin roof, but its slender body had inflicted no apparent harm.

The wreckage of broken limbs and branches lay strewn throughout the clearing between the neighbors' cabins.

The top of one of our loftiest red pines had broken off, been launched through the air like a missile and had punctured the roof of a neighbor's cabin. No one at home there, fortunately.

Another of our grove of proud great pines had lost its grip upon the earth and been pushed over whole. It angled across the road, its top suspended high in a snag of several surviving trees, its uprooted base lifted like a section of pie crust in a too-hot oven.

The trunk of another pine lay prostrate, flat across the road. In its descent to earth it had crushed the bow of an aluminum boat that had been stored upside down by the roadside.

Several black ash in the marsh behind the cove had bent before they broke, their bark a skin stretched into the right angle of the fall. Their interiors were in splinters.

I wanted to survey the aftermath scene from the Point, but the nearer path had been rendered impassable by the trunk and branches of yet another downed pine.

Turning aside from that barricade, I ascended the farther path out to the Point. Arriving on the tip of the Point, what I saw first was what wasn't there—my observation stump. Despite its low profile, cylindrical form, and heavy bulk, it had apparently been blown into the lake. That stump had served me for 34 years, but now it was gone.

The inner shoreline of the cove out to Wolff's Point presented a picket of bared white birch trunks and, where once majestic pines crowned the tip of that point, what faced me now were the black discs of the root clusters...

That evening, while I was back on my own Point again, an osprey passed by, carrying off a fish for its dinner. *Derecho* past, life went on.

The osprey inspired me. A toppled cedar tree lay in the water. Might a fish have discovered that new aquatic structure?

I fetched my rod, cast off the tip of the cedar, and caught a five-pound largemouth bass. . .

The next morning, I paddled into Susan Bay to view the somber scene of broken and mutilated and killed trees.

I passed Hahne Island. Its high and exposed position had made it especially vulnerable to the devastation that would later appear as a page-one photo in the local newspaper.

The shoreline of Susan Bay had been ravaged. Some trees had been pushed over entire, their roots wrenched out of the foothold and exposed into the air; some trees had broken in their middle, snapped clean through; others fell to the weight of a larger neighbor driven down against them; those trees still standing were stripped of limbs and bark. The downed trees all lay pointed in the same direction, as is characteristic of a *derecho* event.

This was a mass slaughter of many individual trees. And yet, the woods as a whole was still there, still green. . .

Back in the area of my cabin, I examined more of the nearby casualties. Some cedars revealed rot in their

*Setting*

heartwood, a weakness that contributed to their victimization by the wind, but the downed pines were solid through and through. The healthy had perished along with the diseased. On the other hand, one dead birch that had stood skeletal for many years remained still standing. . .

After the chain-saw had done its work, I examined the cross section of the pine that had fallen into the snag over the road. I counted the annual growth rings, getting to one hundred well before I touched the outermost layers under the bark.

I was told later that the *derecho* had raised a lake *tsunami* that rolled up a hillside and smacked a cabin and that a great volume of water was pushed out of the lake and down the Pelican River.

The *derecho* of July 4, 1999, I had only heard about while in the general geographical vicinity. For this *derecho* of July 4, 2012, however, I was on the scene, in the direct path, the north shore of Pelican Lake ground zero of the phenomenon.

This *derecho* was destructive to the forest and to human property, but there were no injuries to people, as far as I heard.

Electricity out, it was back to candlelight at night.

In all, a rough time, undergone, endured, and survived.

I set myself to the task of the long and laborious cleanup.

\* \* \* \* \*

Sunset on another early summer evening.

From the Point, I see masses of cumulus clouds spread over the tree line across the southern horizon of the lake. They glow with a golden resplendence in reflection of the sun, which is now out of sight but still sending forth rays to the low-lying clouds.

I sit down on the new observation stump to stare at the transient beauty of the glowing clouds.

The clouds loom as dense bulks, like gigantic animals on haunches. The most massive one looks like the head of a lion full face-on.

A white arc curves over the outline of the lion's mane. Another issues from his right eye. A flash fills his head, as if the sparking of a brain.

Lightning, a summer storm from within the bodies of the beasts. Every second or two now, streaks and flashes erupt at the forefront of the clouds.

No thunder accompanies this lightning, because this storm is very far away, apparently moving east, not north toward me.

The sound of the storm, not thunder then, is made by the waves, impelled by the southwest surface wind breaking over the slope of the tip of the Point, just below me.

This storm is a terrible one, yet, distant as it is and moving by—so different from my recent close experiences of the squall and the *derecho* directly over Pelican Lake—, I can experience it with observational detachment and calm equanimity.

Not so all the local wildlife. The pelicans are heading out on their usual evening foraging, true, but a loon, fleeing the fright of the lightning, flies over my head, making a call of distress. Its mate follows a few seconds later. But where is refuge? And where can refuge be found for dangers more apparent than real?

Directly over my head, before the sun fully set, the sky was a cloudless blue. The storm is truly far away; even so, I felt a drop or two upon my bare arm, stray scattershot.

As the storm progresses in its course, the lightning recedes from the forefront to the depths and backs of the cloud masses, erupting glows rather than sharply defined streaks and flashes.

The storm has been proceeding from my distant right to my distant left, leaving behind it a plain gray sky, the exhaustion.

I have been able to determine the speed of progress of the storm by watching as the component clouds pass certain shore lights. The masses of clouds to the left have been gradually diminishing compared to the plain gray aftermath advancing from the right.

I see the last of the lightning beyond the top of the high promontory of Wolff's Point.

The sky over me is no longer blue, the sun long gone and darkness now settling in.

Nature and her occupying creatures south of my location have been subjected to an intense and severe ordeal of storm, with more than an hour of lightning, as

I have witnessed from afar. Around me and over me, as within me, all has remained tranquil.

The sun now having departed, the planet Venus arrives. Venus shines her steady light.

*****

No moon. All stars.

Stiff breeze. No bugs.

Ah, wonderful!

*****

It is well past midnight. I ease off the observation stump and lie upon my back on the solid rock. I stretch out my limbs into full contact with the earth beneath me.

I look up at the cosmic dome. The multitudinous pinpoints of stars bespeckle the blackness above, an illumination in contrast to the blackness of night around me.

Invisible by day, the universe displays itself at night, to the wonder of the awake; so impressive, so mysterious, an awesome sight for human eyes. At that vision, some become star-struck.

Above the horizon I see the distinctive presence of Mars, shining so brightly that it projects a ray of reflection across the dark surface of Pelican Lake. Below that surface glowing candles rise and fall, shimmering aquatic reflections of the stars' celestial lights.

*Setting*

The star-struck exercise their imaginations in a flight to Mars, with possible colonization there. Imagination becomes will in a *space program*, money poured into the effort to make science fiction fantasies an actuality.

Have we become so alienated from Nature and from our own earthly human nature that we plot an escape from our world of life, off to the inhospitable lifeless environments of those pinpoints out there?

I am a bit cold as I lie upon the rock, but I feel a deeper chill in looking up at the distant stars and planets.

Around me I hear the barking *kronks* of the frogs and the interrogative call of a barred owl. A splash in the cove reports a late-night feeding of a large bass. By dark as by daylight, life is all around me; and I am part and participant of that life.

I look up at the night sky, but I am not star-struck. The wonder and awe I feel is evoked by the multitudinous forms and varieties and dynamics of life here on our earth.

I suffer no fantastic wanderlust for the vast lifeless barrens out there in space. I am fully satisfied with the right-here and with my explorations of the nearby.

# Wildlife

Today there have been swarms of tiny flying insects in such numbers that they have become the most conspicuous component of the environment. They fly about *en masse* and fall upon every surface. The spider who has spent so many days of futile waiting, her fingertips upon the strands of her web, now has a banquet tumble onto her spread. She hardly has time to grab and wrap one, when two or three others fall struggling on other strands.

The most well-known of the mass hatching flying insects is the mayfly, order Ephemeroptera, family Ephemeridae. Ephemeral indeed is the life of these insects, ephemeral, but intense too.

This evening, I looked up from the deck of my cabin at two whirling swarms, one under a high bough of a pine tree, the other a smaller cluster closer to me off the tip of a cedar branch.

Having no specimen within reach, I could not tell what kind of insect they were. No matter. Identification and classification, the labelling and putting-into-a-slot, is less revealing of Nature than is the dynamics of behavior.

Dynamic was the behavior I observed. The aerial assemblages were pulsing swirls of the little bodies. The pine bough and the cedar branch provided sites of rendezvous for orgy.

The hundreds of tiny aspirant lovers in the high swarm and the many dozens in the cluster flew around in a frenzy. Loops and spirals, maybe even figure-eights, soaring, diving, from the outer edge of the mass through its center to the bottom, then turned about and back through the center again. All to find the one among the many. Not a mating dance. A mating air-show.

I tried to follow the course of a single insect through the swarm, but, he so small, so fast, and so far away, it was hopeless. Even my attempt to detect a general pattern in the swarm left me cross-eyed and dizzy. I suppose there is no predetermined choreography for a mating swarm.

The advancing evening reduced the light for observation of the swarm under the high pine bough, but I could still see the cluster off the tip of the cedar branch, the black-dot bodies distinct against the pale sky.

Little by little, the numbers in the cluster decreased, compatible pairs having left to do what can be done only by two, and, perhaps, some fallen from the cluster in utter exhaustion.

At last, only a few were left to continue circling one another. A climax seemed to have been denied them for some reason. Out of so many, no one match for those few unlucky? Whether there are homosexuals and lesbians among the insects I have no idea.

We humans make much art, literature, and music out of our capacity for sexual passion, but I think we may be outdone by the little creatures whose brief lives put a desperation into their passion. Hatch-mate-die is the biography of every living creature. Our human drawn-out hatch-mate-die lives include many years of privation and loneliness, with only occasional moments of the ecstasy of consummation. The ephemeral insects live lives of passion virtually from start to climactic finish.

* * * * *

When I turned on the ceiling globe light in the bedroom, I saw a small spider at the bottom of the bowl of the globe.

How he had entered a closed fixture I wondered, and why, too, because within the rotundity of the globe there was no corner in which the spider could spin a web and set himself up in business.

– – –(Now, as I am writing this, I discover a tiny spider crawling up my shirt, interested no doubt in this narrative about his kin.)– – –

As the two bulbs started their sudden generation of light and heat, the spider now found himself not only in the spotlight, but also in the oven. He twitched in reaction, then ran this way and that on the slippery inner surface of the glass.

He was trapped and doomed, for the only exit and escape was above him, where the two burning bulbs blazed away.

I quickly turned off the light, reached up, loosened the screws that held the globe to the fixture, and pulled the globe down into my hand.

Too late. The spider lay on his back at the bottom of the globe, roasted and scorched, his eight legs contracted in the desiccate stiffness of death.

\* \* \* \* \*

A naturalist is not supposed to go all weepy at the casualties occurring in Nature. The way of Nature is harsh, especially upon the creatures low in the food chain. Prey is preyed upon,—that is how it is. Some few will survive to continue the species.

The naturalist thinks in terms of species within the context of the whole system. As long as the system is healthy, a mass slaughter of individuals is of no concern.

And yet, what about an individual of a species? Is it of no matter that it may suffer some terrible fate? When I think of an individual living creature and all the dire things that may happen to it, I am moved to pity. Yes, pity for the individual. The individual mosquito, let's say.

The individual mosquito starts life as an egg in water. A nice pond or lake would be a congenial environment for a mosquito egg. But some irresponsible females lay their eggs in a remnant of rain in the crook of a tree, there to possibly dry out, or in a puddle in a road, to be run over by a vehicle, or, worse, in a few inches of rain water in a discarded tire,—what a poor start that is!

If the eggs are laid in a pond or lake, a mosquito larva emerges into a dangerous aquatic world. A low-level predator itself, it is surrounded by larger, more voracious predators. Necessarily suspended at the surface to breathe the air, the mosquito larva is vulnerable. Only a *wriggler*, it cannot swim away to escape predators; the wriggling itself attracts fish from below to rise to gobble up the larva.

If, by the luck of sheer numbers, a larva survives to pupa, then to adult, it emerges out of the water. It then takes flight. Ah, flight,—doesn't that enable escape and survival?

No, because the adult mosquito is a weak flyer, easily buffeted by puffs and gusts, headwinds, tailwinds, and crosswinds, forewinds and afterwinds, updrafts and downdrafts, gales, squalls, and windstorms, not to mention tornadoes and those Minnesota *derechos*.

Even in calm, once aloft, the mosquito is quickly attacked by highly maneuverable and efficient aerial killers, the birds and bats. A mosquito may survive its larval stage, only to succumb to the assassins of the air.

The mosquito itself is a pitiful thin and frail creature. How many are crushed and drowned by some torrential downpour?

One not dried to death as egg or consumed as larva or swallowed up in the air survives to a short, bleak life.

A male mosquito makes do sucking plant juices, hardly a diet to encourage one to go on living. As for the female, she has imposed upon her a perilous duty, the finding of blood to nourish the eggs within her.

How can the human indict the mosquito's thirst for blood? The human itself makes the blood flow from cattle, sheep, pigs, and all kinds of fowl and fish. The man cutting into a bloody slab of beef while thinking ill of the mosquito is a hypocrite.

The likelihood of any one female mosquito obtaining the blood she needs is low. If she does happen upon a rare human in the natural environment, that human's skin is likely to be poisoned with a coating of DEET or Picaridin. And the desperate needy female mosquito approaching a human might find sudden death in a slap.

Repelling an individual mosquito doesn't satisfy the human. The human wages chemical warfare on all mosquitoes with DDT (still used in developing countries), pyrethrum, methoprene, malathion and other ever more lethal compounds. The toxins are sprayed on water to suffocate the larvae or fogged in the air to choke the flying adults. They may call it *abatement*, but the human goal toward the mosquito is total extermination.

I knew a sadistic fellow once, who found pleasure in an exquisite method of mosquito murder. He would let a female mosquito pierce his skin. Then, with thumb and forefinger, he would pinch and hold the skin where the mosquito's straw was inserted; he prevented her withdrawal and retreat. His blood pressure would then pump so much blood into the poor mosquito that her body would explode.

Yes, when I consider the mosquito as an individual, I feel pity. The lucky mosquito is the one that lasts long enough to end life in the first hard frost. Most of the others come to a tragic end.

* * * * *

I was seated on a riverside bare slope eating my sandwich, when a green darner alighted on the rock next to me.

The green darner is one of the largest dragonflies. Its ancestors in the early days of life on earth were some of the largest insects ever, their wingspan 30", as we know from fossils.

I saw that the darner was chewing on a small insect it had caught in the air over the river. Unlike my chewing up-and-down on my sandwich, the darner was chewing with jaws side-to-side.

Nor does the darner live hand-to-mouth. Its jaws grasped its meal firmly; the forelegs could be used to grip the lichens on the rock, resisting the breeze that attempted to blow the darner away. The four long, veined, tissue-thin wings trembled in the breeze.

Drawing close to the one who evidently wanted to join me for lunch, looking into the darner's jaws, I could see the two fine antennae of the insect that the darner was chewing upon. I listened for any munching or crunching, but could not hear any sound of the chew.

I drew closer still, almost face-to-face, although, noseless, the darner does not really have what you would describe as a face. It has a flat front over those two scissory jaws. Its eyes appeared as huge clear bubbles with the tiny black spot of its vision inside.

The darner jerked up its head for a closer look at me, first full-front, then a left eye cocked upwards, then a right eye. The movements of its head were robotic, very different from the fluidity of motion of most living and mobile creatures.

Behind its head was the hard case of its thorax, the long tube of its abdomen, and so to its hind end.

*Wildlife*

We mammals have our flesh hung onto our skeletal frame, but the insects reverse the plan, with an exoskeleton enclosing organs within. That makes the bodies of some insects look machinelike, a scurrying beetle like an armored military vehicle crossing the landscape.

I was surprised how the darner's chewing went on-and-on, considering the smallness of its meal. Not a corporal crumb did the darner let drop, so efficient was its method of total consumption.

At last the darner stopped chewing. It then stayed next to me on the sun-warmed rock to proceed with digestion.

I presumed a bit on the short acquaintance of a single shared meal by touching the darner on the back. It did not fly off; it only turned aside and fluttered a bit over the rock to put a bit of distance between us.

I finished my sandwich. The darner too was now done and may have finally had done with me. It took off, hovered a bit, then turned and flew back over the river, seeking the next course of its midday meal.

*****

I was surprised to read that earthworms are considered an invasive species in Minnesota. The glaciers had killed them all off, but now they are back, dumped and let loose by unsuccessful fishermen as excess bait.

Of course, any newly introduced species is likely to upset the previous balance of interactions among the resident species. On the other hand, earthworms aerate and fertilize the soil, or, one might say, they actually create soil as product of their digestive processes. I have always considered the earthworm a most beneficent creature.

My fondness for earthworms is despite the fact that they almost got me arrested.

Earthworms thrive in the black dirt of Illinois. I was packing for a trip to the Boundary Waters once, when an all-day steady soaking rain followed by a cool night set me to thinking about provisioning my trip with fresh-caught Illinois earthworms.

Nightcrawlers are some of the largest earthworms, very scrumptious to smallmouth bass.

Covering a flashlight beam with red cellophane—(for earthworms cringe and withdraw from bright light)—and taking up a coffee can, I ventured into the dark outside my in-laws' house, which, except for myself, had no one home.

On cool wet evenings, nightcrawlers emerge onto the surface to make hermaphroditic love. Half their length extended out of the hole for the tryst, nightcrawlers are vulnerable to quick fingered picking.

As I crept along the house with searching flashlight, stepping oh-so-lightly (because earthworms retreat underground at heavy footfalls), a car pulled up to the curb.

A policeman got out and demanded to know what I was up to. He frowned at my answer and demanded identification, which I did not have on me.

He was about to arrest me as a prowling burglar, when I got an inspiration. I took the officer into the house and identified myself by my wedding photo on the mantel.

And so, I escaped arrest, but, now daunted, I made do with store-bought nightcrawlers for my fishing trip.

The nightcrawlers as bait provoked a smallmouth bass catching bonanza in the Minnesota-Ontario Boundary Waters.

Marveling at their effectiveness, I happened to ask my fishing partner, "Why are the bass here so instantly ravenous for nightcrawlers? There is no way they have ever seen one before in this remote lake."

My partner thought a bit, then said, "What attracts the bass to the nightcrawler is what attracts me to a woman."

"What do you mean?" I asked.

"I mean the plumpness, the wiggle, and the scent," my partner answered, a glint of mischief in his eye.

Some men can't be a day or two in the wilderness without their attention wandering away from the fishing.

The fishing on our Boundary Waters trips generally productive, we never had any excess bait that we might have dumped into the northland.

The Minnesota indictment against earthworms is that they eat the duff. Yes, that they most certainly do. It is their very way-of-life.

The duff provides bedding for the ferns and wildflowers of the north woods. If the earthworms consume all the duff, it is feared that the northwoods ground will become barren, stripped of its blanket of ferns and wildflowers.

And yet, I wonder. Earthworms must find a winter refuge below the freeze line. If only a fraction of an inch of duff overlies solid rock, how could the earthworms burrow down to their long-term survival? My soil survey of the Point convinces me that they'd never make a go of it there.

Now, with global heating accelerating, earthworms cast adrift by failed fishermen in Minnesota may find winters not so harsh and threatening, after all. They may survive in some places and render beneficent services, even if producing something different from what has been.

Whatever the outcome of the case of earthworms in northern Minnesota, the significance is clear: Any life anywhere may be carried off by the human to anywhere else, to survive or perish within the limits of the place to which the alien has been taken. The species of Nature have all become the human's chattels. The consequence will be a gradual homogenizing of Nature and a diminishment of local ecological distinctness. The common canine of the north woods is not the wolf, but the dog.

*****

The water of Pelican Lake is unusually clear this year and low too, despite the 3" rain that I was told fell during the week that I was gone into Canada.

The water clear and low, when I am in my canoe gazing down, it's as if I'm not floating in a boat on water, but, rather, I'm aloft in a dirigible or balloon high over some sandy landscape far below.

Advancing slowly through the shallows of the little cove, I passed over circular depressions in the lake bottom, the diameter of each about the length of my forearm.

Fish beds, but no piscine lovemaking going on. The beds were blanketed—(blanketed, as all beds in northern Minnesota should be)—by lake silt borne in by the waves. Abandoned beds, breeding done with for this year.

But—what was this?—an occupied bed. In one cleaned out, fanned out bowl lay a bullhead, centered in the love-nest.

Why was that bullhead still there? It's sunny July, and all the fishy June lovers have scattered, hungry after the exertions of their generative efforts, intent now on satisfying the more pressing physiological need.

One lone bullhead left behind, still set on the stage for the seduction.

I had an impulse to push the paddle blade down into the bed to see whether the bullhead would stir or flee, but my hovering just three feet above must have been intimidation enough. I refrained from driving away amorous hopefulness.

The fish lay perfectly still in the bed, waiting, waiting. Hasn't the time long passed for any mate to approach, accept the hospitality, and succumb to the seduction?

The ardent lover might just wind up as a frustrated old maid or bachelor. Going through the mating motions, but it may be all futility.

Even so, drive must spend itself, expend itself in discharge, whether futile or fecund.

\* \* \* \* \*

Then, paddling my canoe farther on toward Wolff's Point, I saw something small and silver reflective on the surface of the water. I turned toward it to find out what it was.

A crappie, a few inches long, dead and floating.

I drew the corpse toward me by sculling the paddle. Sliding my hand as a pallet under the little fish, I lifted it up to my eyes for forensic examination.

His body was perfect, as if he should be still alive and swimming.

He seemed too small to have run afoul of a fisherman, and, if anything had assaulted him, there were no perceptible marks of injury. Yet, might he have been struck, shocked, escaped, only to expire? Not all violent deaths provide clear evidence.

Out in the tall aquatic grasses at the tip of Wolff's Point, I heard the croak of a great blue heron.

I paddled over and stared.

Definitely a look of guilt in the heron's feathery face.

The presence of the heron on the scene may have been sheer coincidence, and the tiny crappie would have been too meager a meal for a heron. Nonetheless, suspicion was necessarily aroused. If not guilty of this particular piscicide, the heron is, at least, a notorious repeat offender.

\* \* \* \* \*

A black swimming swarm rotated in a foot of clear water over the sand at the shore of the little cove.

Hundreds of bullheads, each no longer than a fingernail, composed the swarm, which moved as if one organism.

The rotation formed a comma or single quotation mark. Then, drifting sideways, the wriggling mass became roughly rectangular. Another change of direction attenuated the middle to such an extent that the one grouping almost became two. The swarm tightened up again, a few slow-swimming stragglers left behind now whipping their tails vigorously in order to rejoin the vast anonymity.

Which among so many determined the direction and course of all? There did seem to be some hesitancy and cross-purpose initiatives to head some other way. Yet, the swarm held together, by the magnetism of safety-in-numbers. Each tiny bullhead, vulnerable in its singularity, feeling secure in the midst of a vast mass of its fellows.

Still, a bullhead, so prickly with its spines, is no sought-after delicacy for the fish-eaters. A tender crappie would be preferable.

I recalled the bullhead I had seen waiting on the spawning bed some weeks before. Did that one succeed in luring a mate to a spawn, after all? Might these little ones be the offspring or some of the offspring?

I had witnessed only a readiness, not an accomplishment. Yet, accomplishments somewhere there must have been, as this swarm proves.

The engenderment of life awaits no witness. Suddenly, life is teeming all around us, whether we are aware or oblivious.

A swarm of new life, like a mating swarm, appears, as if from nowhere. It throbs with individual and collective vitality. We naturalists are enlivened by that vitality.

\* \* \* \* \*

On my way out to the tip of the Point, I frightened a leopard frog in a patch of grass. The frog in its escape panic took three desperate leaps away from me. The last jump took the frog over the edge of the bluff and down upon Pelican Lake.

The frog kicked and swam, but after a few strokes he disappeared into a great swirl on the surface.

The frog had escaped one who posed no threat, only to perish down the gullet of a ravenous largemouth bass.

\* \* \* \* \*

All day long, a fair-weather gale has blown out of the south. The gale has combined intensity with constancy. Not only was the canoeist deterred, but even the motorboaters stayed indoors, anticipating nothing but abuse out of the air. It is at times of worst weather that Pelican Lake, unmolested by human incursions, has a grasp on its own natural integrity.

Despite the gale, my cabin did not feel well ventilated, even with the windows wide open. Between the cabin and the gale rises the peninsular high rock hill before the Point, an effective windscreen against the south wind.

I saw a birch tree, newly crippled, broken in half by the gale, the living leaves, if not the tree itself, done to death by wind.

I left the cabin and walked over to the shore of the little cove, which was fully open to the big blow.

The wind had pushed the aquatic vegetation out of its element and piled it in a row upon the inhospitable shore. Botanical eviction and homelessness.

Standing on the shore facing the gale was a gull. I expected him to fly off at my approach, but he stood still. When I advanced closer, he put distance between us by walking along the shore. His left wing dragged through the heaped-up waterweeds. A wing broken, perhaps by some mishap related to the gale. He faced the gale stoically, was not in evident distress, but he looked done for as a flyer. He picked something blown onto shore and ate it, a handout from the wind. How will a gull that cannot fly find the food to enable him to live out his natural span?

The water rushed along, some molecules of it that had once suspended on the south shore of Pelican Lake now dashed against its north shore. The waves smacked the boulders of the Point as if out of some seacoast scene.

I was surprised to see two barn swallows flying over the lake, for, not only was the wind a powerful opposition, but wouldn't the flying insects the swallows pursued either be clinging for dear life to some refuge on land, or else, if they did venture out over the water, be promptly whisked back inland?

The two swallows attacked the gale head-on, flying back and forth, up and down over the water. At times, the gale seemed to overmaster them, but, with a burst of speed, the swallows, pushed back toward the woods, powered forward over the water in their sustained foraging effort. What energy they must burn in a struggle against a gale!

Why didn't they show the sense of canoeists and motorboaters? Even gales, the worst of gales, eventually die down, the wind winded. Why not wait it out?

I knew this swallow pair. As last year, so this year they have built their nest under the neighbor's boat canopy at the dock.

I went out on the dock and peered under the canopy. There, upon the aluminum frame, in the corner, under the protective canvas, was the nest. The tiny beaks hung over the edge of the nest in expectancy.

That was why the swallow pair had taken on the gale. Hunger always cries out, whether in calm or storm.

* * * * *

I passed a partridge (i.e., grouse) lying on her belly by the side of the road, flailing one wing.

I stopped the car and got out to check whether she had been struck by a passing vehicle.

As I approached, she stood up and stared hard at me, as if begrudging an interruption.

Then, ruffling her feathers and holding them erect, she hurried across the road, leapt and flew off into the brush.

I think that she had just been dry-bathing in the sand along the roadside, to get rid of mites, as chickens in the barnyard do.

Typical poultry practice.

* * * * *

While I was sitting on the cabin couch, I was startled by a thud of concussion against the building.

I guessed what it was, for there are evidences of just that event accumulated through the forty years the structure has stood here in the woods. Several panes of window glass show cracks caused by that thud of concussion.

The glass of a window, rock hard though it is, is clear,—and so it isn't there. That is, the glass cannot be perceived by a bird whose fast flight is suddenly stopped by the hard wall not seen. The air becomes solid, to a collision sometimes fatal.

I got up from the couch to circumspect the outside of the cabin, to see whether the bird was just injured and might recover, as I once saw a robin after collision stand shaking on the ground below the window, his eyes all flashing stars, until, a few minutes later, he was able to fly off, but without, I think, grasping anything of what had happened to him.

I proceeded clockwise around the cabin, checking the ground below each window for the casualty and looking for any newly cracked pane.

Nothing...until I returned to the front door, where, below the glass panel of the aluminum storm door, lay a grackle. I had stepped over her as I went out.

The door is right next to the couch, which accounted for the effect of the collision upon my seated equanimity.

Many grackles have been about the cabin lately, busy raising the next generation. The young's harsh pleading to be fed is the background cacophony in the environment around my cabin.

The grackle must have hit the glass at full speed, her neck broken by the impact. She hadn't lost so much as a single feather, yet she was certainly dead.

So, a mother grackle gone, her parental nurturance abruptly ended, the burden of her mate doubled, the offspring now having to develop self-responsibility more quickly.

I scooped the grackle up in a dustpan. The body had surprising heft and weight for a bird. Not sentimental about death, I flung the carcass into the woods for natural recycling.

Window glass, which can't be seen, is inscrutable to birds. And when the window reflects like a mirror, it seems to present a rival that must be driven off. One aggressive but uncomprehending male robin launched several weeks of repeated attacks against his own image in a window of our house in Westmont. A futility if ever there was one. He could launch his attack from the branch of a small tree right by the window. The trajectory so short, he didn't build up enough momentum to do himself harm. Even so, he frittered away the breeding season, while real feathers-and-flesh rivals had their way with the neighborhood females.

Whether invisible wall or deceptive mirror, glass is baffling to birds, frustrating, even fatal.

What unseen, uncomprehended barriers or self-reflective illusions baffle us humans? We too crash into the unseen and suffer the deception of thinking we see the other, when it is really only ourselves that we are seeing.

\* \* \* \* \*

The pelican of Pelican Lake is the American white pelican.

I needn't go looking for the bird somewhere over the sprawl of water, for the totem of the lake has a summer settlement close by, on the opposite shore of the narrow Susan Bay, west of my cabin.

There, on a few scattered rock islets, sixty or seventy pelicans reside, along with a company of gulls and an ever-increasing number of cormorants.

Down on a rock islet the pelican is ungainly as it waddles along a few feet from here to there. Its huge long beak makes grooming awkward. So, its homely aspects. But when, as it paddles upon the water, the rising sun shining bright on the whiteness of its feathers, the pelican appears as a sixteenth-century Spanish galleon in full sail. Even I, so poor in imagination, saw that historical mirage.

The white pelican is lumbering in its take-off from the water, a loud splashing of wings, but, once its fifteen pounds are airborne, its wings have power in the stroke. A few strong flaps and the pelican glides over the water.

It can also soar like some great stratoliner. When it sets off to migrate, the flock ascends in a spiral, rising, rising, ever higher, until, attaining the propelling upper winds, the flock is on its way.

The coastal brown pelican dive-bombs for its food. The white pelican's alternate method is to send out the fleet. The hungry ones paddle along together in flotilla, cooperating to drive the fish into the shallows, to be scooped up in the pouched bills.

From the observation stump on the Point, I watched dozens of pelicans floating upon Susan Bay, all of them facing the main lake. Drawing around them and gradually assuming the same orientation were scores of cormorants. More pelicans paddled over to the assembly, more cormorants flew in. Some cormorants at the lead of the column took flight, then the whole flock rose, a mix of large bright whites and smaller blacks.

Flying just above the surface of the water, the column stretched forward across the expanse of main lake, off upon a cooperative feeding foray. Even though the cormorants seemed to lead, I think they merely accompanied, and benefited from, the pelicans' cooperative fishing method.

My earlier references to galleons and fleets sound like oceanic talk about an inland lake. Yet, there is a salt-sea aspect to the pelicans' presence on Pelican Lake. On the rock islets the birds stand on their own *guano*. (I use the Spanish word as the common term.) When you are downwind of one of the islets, as I found myself when I was canoeing, you are subjected to the powerful stench of the acrid urea of the *guano*. Very reminiscent of the ocean shore. (Some tourists to Florida think that it is the salt-sea that they smell, when it is actually the seabird *guano*.)

I haven't yet heard of an enterprising gardener in Orr who has had the idea of harvesting the pelican *guano* as fertilizer for his plants, struggling as they are to grow healthy on rocks in the cold northland.

There have been some summers when, for unknown reasons, the white pelicans never came to Pelican Lake. This lake offers suitable accommodations and plentiful fish;—what more could a pelican want? The pelicans have to put up with the motorboaters, true, and with some gawking birdwatchers, of which I am an occasional one.

Please stay, pelicans, and come back every summer! I don't want to live in a cabin on lost-name lake, where all I could do was stare out and across at empty abandoned bare rock islets.

\* \* \* \* \*

Just outside my bedroom window stands a majestic white pine tree. Stands and has stood since the last millennium. Well, as this is only 2009, that's not saying anything impressive. The tree is certainly a multiple of my own 64 years. Missed by the loggers, it wears the arboreal age spots of moss and lichens.

One hundred measured inches in circumference and maybe as many feet in height, it rises on a massive column, reminiscent of the gigantism of Egyptian or imperial Roman architecture.

Burrowing mammals have made their way into several soft spots at the base; in despite, the pine's foothold seems still secure. Woodpeckers have hollowed out a nest cavity in the trunk, an incursion into the solidity of the heartwood core. The winds and insects have done their ravages, too. This white pine is in the decline of the 200-year lifespan attainable by its species.

Above the halfway point of the upward towering, dead branches and stubs project from the trunk, then, higher up, are living branches green with needles. The very top is a crown of barren branches.

Some of the branches of the bare crown are almost horizontal. Still soundly attached to the tree, they serve this year, as they did last, as a frequent perch for a fellow summer resident, a bald eagle.

From that vantage point on one of the loftiest trees on the shoreline of Pelican Lake, the eagle can survey his domain.

The eagle is not a lord of the realm popular with the other avians. The gulls frequently harass him, and I hear the eagle screaming his protests and threatening retaliation. The osprey too is an enemy of the eagle, bearing grudges due to the many acts of dispossession of fish the mugger has committed against the osprey.

- - -(On the edge of the deck one day, I was startled when something plummeted down through the trees and thumped on the ground in front of me. A headless northern pike, likely the eagle's unsuccessful attempt to rob an osprey.

I went inside my shed, picked up my fillet knife, and prepared an addition to my dinner.)- - -

I myself am favorably inclined toward the eagle's presence. He is, after all, my closest neighbor, he abiding by my abode.

When, in the early morning, I hear him proclaiming himself from his throne on the pinnacle of the pine, I step out to the deck to peek at him over the roofline. If I am still, the eagle tolerates my spying. If, however, I happen to be nosing around in the woods, not knowing of his presence high above me, he becomes suspicious and flies off to one or another of his lofty lakeside perches.

We are like most modern neighbors, I suppose, that is, aware of each other, tolerant of each other's presence, but each minding his own business. We don't have much in common, anyway, he wild and I tame.

The eagle has no need of, or interest in, me. My own desire for neighborly intimacy will have to be satisfied with the touch of two of the eagle's feathers dropped from the perch and come to rest at the base of the great white pine.

* * * * *

I heard the eagle's querulous calls from behind the cabin, more protracted than usual. What was the reason for his upset?

I went outside and scanned the top of the great white pine. I couldn't see the eagle on any of the bare branches, so I returned inside.

The eagle continued his agitated calls. Might he be hurt, in some distress, even down on the ground?

I went out again, listening and looking, looking.

Suddenly, there was a spurt of white spray from a part of the top of the tree concealed from my view. The spray, launched from a hundred feet up, spattered over the area below.

Let that be a warning, birdwatchers. Keep your distance from the vertical.

Anyway, now reassured by the sign of life and evidence of the eagle's continued health, I went back into my cabin.

* * * * *

An eaglet was now perched on the horizontal bare limb of the great pine. An adolescent this one, bulky with plumage, already glaring of eye and armed with the talons and powerful beak of its race.

The parent eagle, my familiar, was on another branch.

When the parent flew off, perhaps in quest of another meal for the young one, a gull moved in to dive-attack the eaglet.

The gull swooped down inches from the eaglet's head. It returned several times to repeat the harassment.

What good was the young eagle's talons and massive sharp beak against the swift maneuverability of the gull? All the young eagle could do was flinch and squeal out a protest at each dive of the gull.

The magnificent eagle! Even the parent eagle is helpless against the harassment of gulls, crows, and jays.

The great—or the perceived great—are laid low by their vulnerability to petty aggravations.

\* \* \* \* \*

Yesterday, as I was out on the Point, I heard behind me something that sounded like trickling water. What, had a spring sprung where there had never been one?

Edging back along the shoreline to the inside curve of the cove, I discovered what the sound was. Mother mallard duck was there with her seven ducklings. All of the seven were slurping up the floating green slime that the wind had blown against the shoreline. Their fourteen beaks smacking the slime made the sound that had me wondering.

Mother duck, not eating, watched over her brood, alert for the safety of her numerous offspring. She took notice of my approach, but did not lead her seven away. As I stood still, watching benignly from a distance, she evidently judged me no danger. She too then joined in on the slurping.

Today, as I paddled out in my canoe, I saw another mother mallard duck. She had with her a one-and-only duckling.

What a contrast between the mother-of-seven and the mother of just one.

The mother and her one-and-only were out in the open water of Pelican Lake.

Suddenly, the duckling paddled in a panic, away from its mother, then abruptly circled back toward her.

I thought that I myself may have been the cause of the fright, although I didn't think that I was that close to the two of them.

Then, swooping down from behind me, the eagle dove to take the duckling.

The mother faced the aerial attack head-on, quacking a resistance. The duckling now cowering behind its mother's protective body, the eagle drew up.

Then he wheeled around for a second try.

Again the mother duck faced the eagle bravely, quacking her fright and concern, but placing herself and her life between her duckling and the eagle's talons.

The eagle swooped by, drew up again, then flew off.

A pair of loons, hearing the mother duck's desperate defense, called out their alarm, for loons too occasionally lose their young ones to eagles.

The difference between a mother duck with a large brood and a duck with few or one may be due not so much to varying fertility as to mothering strategy in a world of duckling-devouring predators.

I have noticed that the mother-of-seven mostly stays close to the shoreline, often leading her brood through the tall reeds and cattails or against the shoreline brush, where an aerial attack from an eagle would be difficult of success.

The other mother had her one-and-only out in open water, where there is no overhead shelter or obstacle to attack.

After the eagle's attempt, the mother duck did lead her little one to shore, the two of them swimming so close that I couldn't see their separate heads for a time. (I briefly wondered whether I had missed the eagle actually snatch up the duckling. I followed in my canoe just enough to verify that the duckling had survived.)

There are better mothers and worse mothers in the animal, as in the human, kingdom. Experience counts, I am sure. But luck plays into it. A mother duck may watch out for eagles, but she cannot see, or protect against, the big snapping turtle or northern pike that lurks below. In some lakes with large muskies, no mother duck, experienced or not, succeeds in raising the next generation.

The instincts of the little ones are a factor, too. The seven bunched close to their mother, but the one-and-only paddled away from its mother, possibly even triggering the attack that almost cost it its life and would have left its mother childless.

It being late July now, the seven are well along, juvenile ducks they seem to my observation. Their mother has done well.

To the other mother I assign no blame. It's a dangerous world for defenseless ducks.

Every single one of the seven might be gunned down by hunters this fall, while the one-and-only duckling may grow up to sire or brood a line that extends into centuries. A mother duck does the best she can. After that, it's a matter of fate.

* * * * *

The mated pair of loons and their two chicks were floating off the tip of the Point. I sat down on the observation stump to observe the family's interactions.

The four of them drifted in the wind, sometimes away from one another, then brought back by paddling feet to their belonging together.

The chicks were bundles of buoyancy, fluffy brown but with the dark heads previewing the blackness of their maturity.

They displayed some of the mannerisms of adults:— When resting, they would lay their head upon their back and its warmth. They would lean on their side and kick and wave a leg in the air, as if to dry it.

(Except for the period of nesting, a loon's feet are always wet.) And they would rise up on their feet and flap their wings in rehearsal for their future of flight. However, their faint nasal *hnn* gave no hint of the high-volume vocalizations they will be capable of as adults.

The family drifted into the cove. The parents then began to dive for fish to feed the chicks.

Loons float so low in the water that their dive is more like a swift and smooth submersion. There is nothing common about the common loon. The loon well merits its alternate name, *great northern diver*.

The shallow cove is full of fish; the loon parents brought one up on every second or third dive. Upon surfacing, the parent would crush the little fish in its strong beak, softening it, then swim toward one or the other of the chicks. The hungry chick would paddle forward to get the food. The parent would present the fish upon the surface, crushing and softening it some more to make it easy to swallow. The chick having consumed, the parent would then dive for the next course.

The parents brought up one fish after another to their two offspring. With such superabundance of supply, all went so easy.

After a while, the chicks did not swim so eagerly to the offered food; the parent had to seek out a chick to feed. One chick seemed reluctant to eat more; the other even turned away. At that, the parent ate the fish.

The chicks now fed and full, they swam to their mother and drew alongside her for body contact. One chick tried to climb atop its mother's back, as it had done for warmth in its infancy, but now it was so big that it slid off the mother's side. It made a few more clumsy attempts. The mother tolerated them, but then, having had enough, she dove. Infantilism had to be left behind.

When their parents dove, the chicks would put their heads down into the water, as if looking for the source of their food. One chick attempted a dive, kicking hard, but its rump remained on the surface. The second try went better; it was subsurface, not deep, but at least a brief full submersion.

After a period of rest—not so long that one would think full digestion had been accomplished—, the parents did some more dives, brought up more fish, which the chicks accepted. I fancied that the chicks were bulking up before my eyes.

Indeed, when the chicks drifted away from their parents and closer to me at the Point, I saw that their bodies viewed from above looked like a thick potato pancake. When one chick rose on its feet to exercise its wings, the white belly had a plumpness verging upon obesity, like the bottom-heavy penguin. How well fed the two chicks were!

The chicks were now much closer to me than to their parents, but neither of the parents seemed anxious about that. The father even swam over to bring a small bluegill to a chick.

He gradually led the chicks back to the open water and to their mother. The family then drifted off away from me.

Having provided food for the chicks, the father paddled a short distance from the other three. He was now an alert sentinel, watchful and protective.

Unlike ducklings, which are "raised by a single mother", loon chicks enjoy the survival advantage of a shared parental dutifulness.

* * * * *

A young merganser paddled over to the parent, approached and bent low in the food-begging posture.

The parent turned away.

The young one persisted, following and begging.

The parent then drove the young one off.

Surprised and baffled, the young one returned to attempt yet another begging for food.

Now the parent rose up and launched what almost seemed like an attack, driving off the juvenile again and again over an expanse of water.

At last the young one understood and paddled away. Parental duties had come to an end. The young one had been taught how to catch fish, how to feed itself. It was on its own now.

* * * * *

The osprey leapt from a treetop and glided down over the lake.

Flying just above the water, she dipped and dragged her feet just under the surface, cutting a straight sharp line through the water. She rose up slightly, flew along, then did another dip-and-drag. Then up and out, down back in, the dip-and-drag repeated six times across the expanse of lake.

I did not see that osprey catch a fish. I did not see her eat a fish. Even so, I know that that osprey caught and ate a fish.

I saw her wash feet and talons after a fish meal.

\* \* \* \* \*

High above me, a falcon was in pursuit of some swallows that were in pursuit of mosquitoes.

The falcon picked out one of the swallows and swooped from behind for the kill.

The swallow twisted and fluttered in erratic aerial maneuvers, whether to catch insects or to elude the falcon I could not tell.

The swallows disappeared beyond the horizon tree line, the falcon following.

I didn't witness the ultimate outcome, but my impression was that swift falcon would not succeed against acrobatic swallow. As for the insects, they had no chance.

In another predator-prey incident, I saw yesterday our resident osprey hover, then plunge to the water with a great splash, only to regain flight, shake off water, then fly away with empty talons.

Many are the failures that the hunter must overcome; tenacious must be the perseverance possessed by those that live by taking lives never freely given.

\* \* \* \* \*

The same heron that fishes the small patch of stand-up grasses off Wolff's Point also takes up his stalking station in the more extensive area on the inside of the cove between Wolff's Point and my own Point.

The aquatic grasses and reeds as tall as the heron and he not at all showy (plain gray despite his name, Blue) and stock-still besides, it is not easy to see him without binoculars.

And so, I didn't see the heron at first as I was fishing the shoreline facing him.

I was casting a topwater prop-bait, hoping that my little contrived splashes would provoke a large splash of an attacking bass.

I heard a loud splash, or ploosh, but it came not from the area of my lure, but from the cove shoreline.

Deer occasionally emerge from the woods in the evening for a drink of water out of Pelican Lake. The ploosh was made by a young doe.

After her drink of water, she was amusing herself in a frolic. She would raise her front hooves and dash them down into the shallow water, apparently just to enjoy the sound of the splash. Then, twisting about, she made a few leaps for a series of splashes. She ran a bit along the shore, stomping for the sounds of the splashes, then wheeled around in a twist and leapt and stomped and splashed some more.

It was fun, not a bath, that the doe was after, for she carried on her gambols in a few inches of water, keeping most of her body dry.

The doe's commotion displeased the heron, who, so nearby, was having his fishing ruined. He slowly strode away from the doe and her delinquent violation of the calm and quiet so necessary for fishing.

The doe continued her splashing, tireless in the enjoyment of her simple self-entertainment.

Out in the lake, a Canada goose approached a landing. As soon as she set down, she straightaway began to paddle toward the doe and the heron.

The goose sailed a purposeful straight line, as if she were late for a get-together and hurried to arrive before the dispersal of her meeting-mates.

By now, the heron had put some distance between himself and the doe and her noise and nuisance. Yet, irritated as the heron was, he did not up and fly away. After all, he had dinner to catch, and he was standing on his prime fishing ground—or muck as it was.

The doe could snack in her play, as now and then she would pull a birch leaf off a tree hanging over the water and eat it.

She found a piece of shiny silvery paper, some trash floated by the winds into the shore. She picked up the paper in her teeth and tossed her head, waving the paper as if as signal flag to her kin back in the woods. Being deer not goat, she disdained the eating of paper foil. She dropped it, returning it to its career as litter.

The goose had now arrived at the edge of the stand-up grasses. Why she had gone there so directly, so purposefully, I could not guess. No goslings to defend that I could see. She must have been attracted by the doe's frolic.

And so, there they were together, the heron, the doe, and the goose, a strange trio in assembly.

There is the stress and danger of *the struggle for survival* in the natural world, true. However, among a fish-eater, a browser on terrestrial vegetation, and a grazer on aquatic and terrestrial salad, there was nothing to fear.

Every now and then, there occurs a harmless going-along and getting-along among the other species sharing our world of life.

* * * * *

My nearby neighbor had told me that he saw a black bear right outside his window last week. "And it was a big one, too."

Returning on the path from fishing on the Point this morning, I encountered my neighbor standing on his porch.

"I didn't see your bear," I said to him, "but I found evidence of your bear. He dropped a load right on the path. Fresh."

"I wonder why he's hanging around," my neighbor said. "There's nothing for him to eat around here."

There must be *something*, for I had found the proof of two meals in the scat. First out was a bulk of brown fibrous material, then, the next course, bright shiny green spinachy leaf. The scat was very moist, not only from the rain, but also from the recentness of the deposit.

Taking up a small stick, I probed the scat. (Analytic curiosity. Romantic nature-lovers might forgo such close scrutiny.)

My probing revealed that there were just the two types of vegetative meals in the deposit. My probing also raised an aroma, but that was not so repulsive as might be expected. It is the excrement of meat meals, not of processed plants, that raises a stink.

The scat was already occupied by insects setting about the recycling. Most conspicuous were several thumbnail-size beetles, black, with two parallel yellow sections on the head. They were, if not the famous *dung beetles*, at least deserving that description without specific appellation.

The beetles were burrowing into the bear scat.

I found two of them coupled up, combining fornication with a feast in a setting to a human's distaste but apparently not to theirs.

As the archaeologist excavates old trash piles to learn about the human, so the naturalist probes scat to learn about animal life processes. In scat, the bear both bares the fact of his existence and displays his diet.

A bear that happened to pass by the site of his last bowel movement, only to find a naturalist bent over the pile in a probe, would certainly puzzle over the perversions of the human.

"It's a search for knowledge," the naturalist would tell the bear. "Thanks for your cooperation...."

Then there's the old riddle:

Question: "What's the worst thing you can find in bear scat?"

Answer: "Buttons."

\* \* \* \* \*

In my writing of *guano,* excremental spatter from on high, and scat, you might be wondering whether I have coprophilic tendencies or am one of those adults who still indulge in pre-adolescent gross humor.

No. As much as I would like to maintain a tone of wholesomeness throughout this book, organic crudities are as much a part of conveying the natural world as are lyrical purple prose and appreciative aesthetics. More practically, you're never going to actually see all the animals in an environment. So, you have to be alert to any evidences of their existence, of which scat is one.

How difficult would it be to conduct a census of all the species of life-forms in the northwoods environment?

The microlife here may be revealed by a magnifying glass or microscope, instrumental means to discovery that I seemingly disparaged before. Just dig in the duff. The tiny creatures cannot escape your scrutiny and survey.

The plants stand still for your inspection, identification, and registration. You can easily tally the tree species. No problem there.

Most insects are in such superabundance that you'll have little trouble drawing up a list. Some of them will even seek you out.

A survey of aquatic life-forms should not be a difficult undertaking. My Pelican Lake is a rockbound basin. All that lives in the water is in that basin. It's just a matter of dipping or angling.

The birds proclaim themselves in song, especially in the spring. If you've listened to tapes of birdsongs, you could identify the species present without glimpsing them flitting through the dense canopy; bird listening may be more productive than bird watching. If you can identify the characteristic nest structure of a species or recognize its fallen feather or eggshell, you'd be further along in your census. Waterfowl are in the open to show themselves. As for those tiny elusives in the treetops, well, you might have to resort to binoculars for them.

Some creatures present are permanent or seasonal residents, some are only transients (just passing through). Birds can fly anywhere, after all, and they sometimes do. They may suddenly appear in a place they have never been seen before, like that roseate spoonbill in St. Paul; those are vagrants. Irruptives are birds driven from their home range by hardships of lack of food or severe weather. Transients, vagrants, and irruptives are anomalies, not to be included in the census of residents.

Besides transients who come and go, there are other animals whose permanent range is now extending northwards into the north woods. I expect snowshoe hares, but here come the cottontails. Not the Canada jay, but the blue jay. Conversely, northland mammals that should be here I have never seen,—a pine marten, a fisher, a wolverine. Any census of northwoods creatures is provisional, changing with the changing climate.

The north woods is a vast expanse. As you cannot inspect every square foot of it, it would be unreasonable to require your census of life-forms to be absolutely complete. (In any environment, there may be undiscovered creatures, no less in a backyard than in the interior of the Amazon rain forest or the depths of the sea.)

In carrying out your census of the northwoods life-forms, you will find difficulties when it comes to the mammals. Many of them are nocturnal, some by nature secretive.

Lying in bed, you hear something scurrying about outside the window. You get up, turn on the light, and look outside, but it is already gone. What was it?

Mammals that are vulnerable, without defenses, will hide from you. Predators, usually stealthy, owe their survival and success to avoiding being seen. Animals must move around, true, but bumping into them is only happenstance. It is not easy to stalk the wary or stalk the stalkers.

To draw up your list of the mammals in the northwoods environment, then, you will need to be alert to evidentiary tracks and signs.

A track in mud is a footprint that serves as a fingerprint. An animal's presence may be discovered in a tree trunk rubbed raw (a buck deer in rut), bark scraped from a tree above the height of a man (a bear), or a rotten downed trunk ripped open for ants (a bear again). A path from a lake or river through pressed-down grasses is revelatory (a beaver).

That sulfurous stink lingering in the air is an identification giveaway.

Scattered remnants of a consumed meal indicate the eater, as does the next day's scat. You might find nest, lodge, burrow, or den and infer from those the occupant. Existential evidence may be drawn from the food, the shelter, and the clothing too,—a sharp quill or a patch of shed fur perhaps.

Finally, unpleasant but common, you may come across the corpse of the animal itself, fallen in the area of its haunts or as road kill. It is unfortunate that much of our knowledge of the existence of the animals around us is from road kill.

By all of these forms of evidence, you can know that an animal is present, even without actually seeing it. Spying on an animal is an intrusion into its life, anyway. And we should have gotten beyond the old practice of proving an animal's presence in an environment by shooting it and turning the carcass over to the taxidermist.

\* \* \* \* \*

Of course field guides already contain a census and check-list of the life-forms of the north woods. Even so, taking on a census as a personal project might be a worthwhile discovery experience, provided that you don't deceive yourself that all that tallying will add up to any deeper understanding or more keen awareness.

I have found amusement in the ways of bird watchers, *birders* as they call themselves. Each birder has a *life list* of all the kinds of birds personally seen. Birders are competitive with one another on that list. "I have 286 birds on my life list," one birder boasted to me. Now, if you picked up a phone directory and read off 286 names, could you claim that you know 286 people and can tell me all about them and the community they live in?

I once tagged along on a bird-watching walk, on which eleven binoculars were accompanied by twelve people. (I went plain-eyed.) "Look, a spotted sandpiper!" one birder exclaimed. "No, that's a solitary sandpiper," another contradicted. The two of them then got into an argument back-and-forth, based upon the details of the bird seen through the binoculars. Why so contentious on the identification? Well, maybe one had a nagging vacancy in the life list just waiting to be filled on that particular day of the life.

Regarding life-forms, I believe that if you grasp the basic nature of sandpiper that's good enough. The noun is an adequate identification; you might get all cross-eyed over the differentiating adjectives. Identification is all just *itness*, anyway.

I don't devalue knowledge-for-itself, but I am against the knowledge as commonly taught in classroom biology. I feel myself fortunate that I never took a biology class in which I would have been forced to dissect a frog. That detached analytic—(and I am not at all squeamish)—would have put me off any appreciation of living frogs in Nature. The academic study of biology may have estranged as many people from Nature as has our modern mass removal from a natural environment, biosphere, to the artificial one, technosphere.

A detached analytic of *itness* is a methodology suitable to automobile mechanics, but it is the wrong approach to Nature.

Nature is not an *it* out there. Nor is Nature a collection of *its*. One Minnesota-specific field guide series offers the following volumes: Wildflowers (200 varieties), Wild Berries and Fruits (165 kinds), Trees (93 kinds), Fish (75), Birds (111), Ducks, Geese, and Swans (59), and Mammals (75). Find and see specimens of all those. Now, do you know the all of Minnesota Nature? (We must except species of microlife and insects as practically countless and maybe uncountable.)

As with the birdwatchers, not much is to be gained by scorekeeping, the quantitative that never adds up to a qualitative.

You don't really know these north woods until you settle in to the setting, become attuned to the all of the environment,—the aura, not the weather, the forest, not the trees, the lake, not the water, the community, not the individual specimens.

Nature is the dynamic of our own life within as deeply related to, participating in, the larger complex dynamic of the community of life.

So, enroll yourself on the census of life-forms, put yourself on the life list.

* * * * *

Using the range maps in a field guide, I thought that I would draw up a census list of animals that are generally absent from the north woods. To stay within the possible I would limit my list to the array of mammals living in the state of Minnesota. And I would consider the reasons why those certain animals are not, or cannot be, here in the boreal forest.

My list:

Top of the census list of the absent is the badger. The badger is a champion excavator, but, even if it had claws of steel, the badger would not be able to dig a den out of the solid bedrock here.

Nor could the three Minnesota species of ground squirrels or the two species of pocket gophers scratch out a burrow or network of tunnels through granite. No place to live, they cannot live here.

Same for the eastern mole. Now, the star-nosed mole is commonly above ground or in the shallow subsurface, so it might make it somewhere here in the north.

The woodchuck would seem to face the same stony obstacle as the badger, but the woodchuck is more flexible in his shelter requirements. He might make do with a den in a roadside cutting, or, as I found him on a fly-out fishing trip into Ontario, as neighbor under the cabin porch.

Anyway, first reason why some mammals are not here in the north woods: "This is the land of rock."

If I ever see an opossum hereabouts, I will know that global heating has well advanced, because the opossum's pink nose, exposed ears, and bare tail would expose it to frostbite and general suffering if it were to try to endure the far-northland severe winter.

The harsh climate is the second reason for the exclusion of certain animals. (One February day, 1996, in Tower, Minnesota: -60° Fahrenheit.)

A few species of mice abound in the north woods, but we householders won't have to deal with the common house mouse. Even if the house mouse got into the shelter of a cabin, it would be in for a rude surprise when the humans there did the end-of-season shutdown and departed, the now unheated cabin turning into a winter icebox. Then, too, the house mouse has become accustomed to a diet of gourmet foods provided by the human. The northwoods larder is meager and skimpy.

Nor would the gray squirrel, an urban, suburban, and parkland resident, thrive on the spare diet of seeds from pinecones, as our indigenous little red squirrel can.

Lack of adequate food makes living off the land here as challenging for some animals as it would be for a human.

When winter removes food resources by freezing over lakes or killing off the insects, the waterfowl and insectivorous birds can just fly off. The mammals are not capable of such a quick and easy relocation. If their food supply suddenly disappears, they starve.

I would expect raccoons in the north woods; they are well-furred, hardy, and omnivorous. However, I suspect that, like the house mouse and the gray squirrel, the raccoon has been spoiled by the human. Cornfields on the farms and garbage cans in suburbs are more appealing to a raccoon than the slim pickins of the deep woods menu.

Resisting and surviving the humans' extirpation attempts, all the wild canines and wild felines will be on the census of the present, rather than on the census of the absent. They live primarily in the open, are fully furred against the cold, are tough against all environmental rigors, and find an adequate supply of warm-blooded meals in the woods.

But prairie animals like the jackrabbit and the pronghorn would be just as out of place in the north woods as an alligator would be.

Every life-form has its basic requirements, which, if not met, exclude it from an environment. Northland rock, climate, and scarcity of food (year-round or seasonal) are all exclusionary.

In all, the north woods is an ecosystem deficient in hospitality.

* * * * *

The end-of-the-road neighbor told me that she has become afraid to continue taking her usual morning constitutional walk on the road through the woods.

Why?

She said that someone somewhere near here sighted a cougar.

A mountain lion in the Minnesota woods?

One of the more startling bits of TV news I heard in recent years was the report of a cougar gunned down by the police in a Chicago alley.

We have so crowded the wild creatures that they have no place to go except among us. Still, I'm skeptical about the local cougar sighting. Bobcat more likely, or lynx just possibly.

It used to be the newly aggressive black bears that the local hikers were anxious about. The black bear is a true longtime Minnesota native. But now a *lion*?

It is the wild animals that aren't there that may arouse the most fear.

. . . And yet, another person just now claims to have seen the cougar, remarking the black tip of its long tail.

Am I in danger in Minnesota, as if I were in Chicago?

# Animal Encounters

A shroud of fog hung over Pelican Lake at dawn. The surface of the water lay flat and smooth under the stillness.

I roused myself, got dressed quickly, took up my fishing rod, and headed down the path to the tip of the Point.

My chosen lure for early-morn bass fishing was a soft plastic green frog, as realistic in its motions as in its general appearance.

I cast out the frog and gave it a few provocative twitches.

The surface of the lake erupted, once, then again. (It was rare for a bass to miss such an easy target on the first try.)

As I set the hook, I felt the fish briefly, then the fish was off. I reeled in the empty line. Frog gone. Had I failed to tie a secure knot?

I quickly returned to the cabin, hooked up another fraudulent frog, and returned to the tip of the Point. I cast out again, and—(my mistake)—to the same spot as my first cast.

Another explosion on the surface, another take, a *tic*, and my second frog was gone. Again I reeled in the empty line.

I felt the end of the line. It had not broken; it had been cut. Not by a bass; it must have been the very sharp-toothed northern pike that had cut my line.

I scanned the surface of the water, hoping that the pike that had cut the line missed or ejected the frog, which would float back to the surface. But no, there were no floating frogs for me to retrieve when they would later blow back to shore or perhaps I could launch my canoe to fetch.

No bass caught, two lures lost to a voracious northern pike,—the same one I presumed.

I was momentarily demoralized at the futility of my fishing and the loss of my only two very effective frog lures.

But then I took action.

I hurried back to the cabin once again, attached an uncuttable wire leader to the line and then put on the first lure at hand, a balsa minnow.

What were the odds that I could catch the pike that had robbed me twice? Wasn't his belly now so full with the bulk of two frogs that he withdrew to the deep to digest?

Slight chance, but I would try anyway.

I knew the northern pike as a gluttonous predator, one that may start digesting before he has even fully swallowed. I once saw the hind part and tail of a northern pike sticking out of the mouth of another northern pike that was not much bigger than what he had just eaten.

I cast to the same spot. What had been my mistake with the second frog would be my strategy for the attempted retrieval of both frogs.

Reeling the balsa minnow back in, I felt a drag on the line. Not weeds, as I first thought, but a northern pike that soon revealed itself. That fish that would be my lunch.

I landed the pike upon the rock of the Point and took him to the cleaning table.

As I filleted him I felt two bulges in his belly. Opening the pike up, I squeezed out of his stomach the second frog, then the first frog. I then carried the frogs and the cleaned fillets to the cabin.

What insatiable hunger in the northern pike! A hunger that turned out to be the vulnerability that enabled me to satisfy my own hunger.

\* \* \* \* \*

A large painted turtle was paddling his subaqueous way along the shoreline of the Point, as I stood fishing there.

His head, now submerged, now emerging, was directed toward the land, as if, amphibious though he is, his interest and orientation were toward the land.

He worked his way along the shoreline and around the Point, as I too worked the Point, I a definite terrestrial, but, when fishing, my own interest and orientation toward the water.

The turtle and I kept facing each other, now to the

left, now to the right, like slow-dance partners.

As close as we were, the turtle showed no fear of me. It almost seemed that he wanted to climb ashore and make my acquaintance. Very sociable for a cold-blooded creature.

His overtures, if such they were, distracted me from my fishing. Why should I be in futile pursuit of something, when something else experiential was offering itself to me?

Forgetting the fish, my attention shifted to another quarry, the turtle, although I intended no harm. Approaching, he seemed so approachable; why not snatch him up?

As the turtle drew close to a sloping shoreline rock, I laid aside my fishing rod and slowly came down to him.

He turned away, but not in any perceptible fright, and paddled slowly along the shore.

I followed and stalked him.

Again he put his foreclaws upon a sloping shoreline boulder. Blinking at me, he held there in perfect calmness.

I descended toward him with slow controlled steps. Surely as I got close, he would wheel about and power down to safety in the depths. But no, he just stayed, facing up at me.

Still expecting him to flee human contact, I took slow crouching step after slow crouching step, wondering what exact distance of intrusion would provoke his retreat and escape.

I calculated the length of my arm and the proximity required for a successful grab.

Then, close enough, I lunged with left arm, pressed the turtle against the boulder and snatched him up, the span of my hand just wide enough to embrace his shell.

What a fine healthy specimen of painted turtle he was.

I backed up the slope and sat down on the observation stump to make his intimate acquaintance or to examine him as a naturalist. (I wasn't sure whether my purpose of his apprehension was for society or science.)

Anyway, he was a well-formed specimen of his race. A perfect shell, carapace and plastron (the top and bottom of any turtle,—I did want to get to know him top to bottom). No moss or fungus on the shell, the plates all firm and clean.

Getting to know the turtle's shell was only a superficial acquaintance, of course. I had to look him in the eyes, which I did, although, his sociability gradually deserting him, he withdrew into his shell. His receding head was garish in its yellow striping, so provocative in one who had now become coy.

I happened to notice under his left foreleg an infestation of small leeches. As compensation for my rude abduction, I decided to render him a medical service.

I drew from my pocket a fishing tool, a hook remover. Inserting its tip into the shell's chamber for the turtle's foreleg, I snapped the alligator jaws of the tool upon the leeches one by one and pulled them from their parasitism, dropping them to their expiration upon the dry rock. Once I feared that I had pinched the turtle's flesh instead of a leech, but the turtle showed no hurt, remained impassive.

I thus freed my new friend from a half-dozen bloodsuckers. One tiny leech, down deep in the folds of the turtle's skin, had to be left there, lest I violate the first rule of the Hippocratic Oath: "Do no harm to the patient."

The turtle's head remained inside, as I performed my medical ministrations. He had neither hissed nor attempted to bite, as turtles are wont to do when molested. I was not a molester. Just a kindly helper, like Androcles with the lion.

I set the turtle down in a little cavity at the tip of the Point. Although the turtle now had his feet in water and a passing motorboat even churned up waves that splashed his face, the turtle showed no urgency to escape back to his freedom.

His head was slow to emerge from the shell. When it did so, he looked out at the lake, not back at me, his aggressive benefactor.

At last, apparently having had enough of the land and its creatures, the turtle propelled himself down the slope and dove into disappearance in the underwater world of Pelican Lake.

\* \* \* \* \*

That turtle gone, I remembered another one, in a different setting, an Illinois forest preserve pond, an encounter I wrote about at that time, as follows:

Winter has been undone. First, there was the week of nighttime temperatures that never went below the 32° freeze-point. Then, days of daytime temperatures in the 50°s, with rain that beat down the accumulated snow. Next, bright sunny days in the 60°s, the snow all disappeared and the ponds and lakes ice-free. Yesterday, more sun and strong warm southern winds, the high 70°s. Today, similar, nearly 80°, summery.

The cattails on the fringe of the pond had their dried stalks broken and beaten down by the winter winds and pressed flat by the weight of the snow. Now they lie exposed like a ragged mat. You can step upon them and approach the shore of the pond, at least as close as to where the water of the sodden earth rises at the weight of your body through the mat and up the sides of your shoes.

Exploring along the shoreline of the pond, I saw on the cattail mat a turtle facing the fully thawed pond water about two feet from entering. The turtle was drawn into its shell.

In the Mardi Gras of life, the turtle is taken as a party-pooper. He is moping and dragging and seemingly sullen too. But he is not sullen. Cold-blooded, the turtle is susceptible to the vitality-depressing effect of the temperature conditions, whether of air or water, within which he must live and try to thrive. When his ambience is cold, he withdraws into his shell, not sullen but just prudently conserving his life force.

I approached the turtle slowly, stepping as lightly on the cattail mat as I could, so as not to alarm him into flight. He was a half-grown painted turtle, not so big that I couldn't grasp him with one hand.

I took hold of the turtle from the top of his shell. When you pick up a turtle, you must grasp the shell just down to its rim, for, if your fingers extend below, the turtle's hind leg will claw your little finger, the foreleg claw your forefinger, which will likely cause you to drop him. You must also keep your fingers away from his head, lest he thrust out his head and bite you.

Lifting the turtle up, I expected to feel the surge of his attempted escape, head extended, legs flailing, even the tail whipped back and forth, as if that little appendage could aid the acceleration toward freedom.

I had the turtle captured in my grip, but I felt no surge to escape. He remained still and withdrawn.

I turned him over for examination.

I saw his tail tucked in to the left, his hind legs and forelegs all tucked in. The underside of his shell looked as clean and perfect as the top.

Then, turning him back right side up, I looked at his head, visible even though tucked in like the rest of his extremities and extensions.

I felt a stab of pathos in recognition. Both his eyelids were sunk into the eye sockets. I remembered that sight from a day with a pet turtle in my boyhood. This turtle too was dead.

There were no signs of organic decay, no stench of putrescence, nothing to indicate death except those sunken eyelids and the stonelike stillness of the turtle in my hand.

I put the turtle back down where he had been, facing the pond and what would have been the environment of his next summertime. He had emerged from the ultimate cold of hibernation and struggled down to the continuation of life, only to fail two feet short of it.

I looked at the hand I had used to pick up the turtle. I did not see there any uncleanness to be wiped off on my pants or washed away in the still-frigid water of the pond.

I moved on in further exploration of winter turned into spring.

* * * * *

Have I just violated my earlier resolution to keep this book ice-free and snow-free, letting an Illinois chill intrude? Well now, back to summer in Minnesota. . . .

I was spray-washing the spider webs off the side of the cabin with a garden hose, when a deer mouse dashed from the undergrowth and headed under the cabin.

On perverse impulse, I directed the spray at the mouse, dousing his hinder parts just as he reached the cabin substructure.

Why blast the "wee, sleekit, cow' rin', tim'rous beastie," so harmless and inoffensive? Well, he is *vermin.* Besides, if today under the cabin, maybe tomorrow inside the cabin.

My cabin hadn't been occupied for a few years, so, when I took up residence, the first thing I had to do was get the mice out. Two of them ran around as if they owned the place. I laid two traps down and turned off the light of the room they were in. It wasn't but a few minutes that I heard one trap go off. So I caught the first one. I thought I'd better remove him, lest his visible corpse be a warning to the other one. I turned on the light, and there was Mouse Number Two still all brazen in front of me. How could I go into the room and remove Mouse Number One without scaring away Mouse Number Two? I stood in the doorway, waiting for Mouse Number Two to turn his back. Instead, he scurried right past the corpse of his partner, headed for the second trap and tried to take the bait,—just ignoring me completely. The trap got him, not with a loud snap, because northern mice have more bulk of body, but a firm-enough clampdown. And then I had my own cabin back to myself alone.

Mice have long cohabited with humans, but, for our part, we have done all we can to oust the trespassing intruders.

It is said that, "If you make a better mousetrap, the world will beat a path to your door." Actually, existing mousetraps are effective enough, if employed properly. I have enough mouse-catching experience to inform and enlighten those who wish to rid themselves of rodents. I have learned from a master.

The methodology he taught me: For hardware, the old standby Victor mousetrap with the bear claw bait holder, spring, and crushing clamp. Cheese is the stereotypical mouse bait, but cheese dries out, loses its odor and crumbles. Instead, I pry open the bear claw bait holder, insert half of a peanut and gently clamp it, being careful not to break the peanut, then coat bait holder and peanut with peanut butter, which is deliciously odoriferous and holds its form and allure. The mouse may lick off the peanut butter without springing the trap, but when he then tries to pull out the peanut, he will surely depart this earth.

And so, the manual of instruction.

The learner is entitled to know the experiential basis of the teaching. Also, trapping furbearing mammals such a part of northwoods lore, there are stories to be told. I hereby chronicle true tales told to me:

### "Adventures of a Mouse Catcher"

My master, the old trapper, speaks:

"Well, you see now, if you know what you're doing, you'll catch the mice you want to get rid of...but you never know what you might find in the trap.

"What if you find nothing? The bait is still there, but the trap is sprung. What happened? You want a trap with a hair-trigger, sure, but—you know what?—a drop in temperature at night might have contracted the metal and sprung the trap. Not many people know that that can happen, but it does.

"Now, if the trap is sprung and the bait is gone, well, the mouse took the bait and got away. You didn't set the trap right.

"Don't give up. You know what? A mouse that takes the bait and gets away scot-free is the most catchable mouse there is. Why? Because he's sure to come back to the same place for another free lunch. And his caution will be gone; he'll let down his guard. So, set the trap right and you'll get 'em.

"I always get 'em. I got two-for-one once. That's right. Two brother mice stuck their heads in at the same time, and—wham!—they died together.

"I get 'em and I get 'em all. I was at a fishing outpost cabin once. It was September, and all the fishermen that had been in the cabin through the whole summer just left their snacks lying around, so careless, that the cabin was infested. It took me two nights, but I cleaned the cabin out. Thirteen dead mice, then all clean and quiet.

"Another thing. I say don't reuse a mousetrap. Besides it ain't sanitary, repeated use weakens the spring. I was out checking traps with a maintenance man once. We came across a trap with a mouse in it,—clamped in his middle, but so alive that he was running in place, like on one of those treadmills for hamsters. The spring of the reused trap was too weak to crush the mouse dead. The maintenance man drowned the poor thing in a bucket of water.

"I've had a few botches myself, I confess. Nobody's perfect in the mouse-catching business. I went to check a trap in my shed once. It was gone. Now, a rat or a squirrel might carry off a mousetrap,—that's one possibility for why a trap goes missing. I set about a search. At the other end of the shed, I found my trap, with a mouse in it, still alive, caught by the tail. Wrong end! I was too tenderhearted to beat the poor creature to death. You know what I did? I baited another trap and slid it nice and easy toward the mouse, figuring he might be hungry again. Sure enough—some never learn—, he took the bait and ended his life. So, there were two mousetraps for one mouse, where earlier I told you about two mice in one trap. I guess it'll all come out even in the end.

"I once caught a bat in a mousetrap. Yes, a bat. Well, a bat is just a mouse with wings.

"You never know what you might find in a trap, I said before. One time I picked up a trap with its dead mouse, and I noticed that the mouse had a hole in its chest. That's right, a hole. While he was lying dead in the trap, some other creature—mouse, mole, shrew, I don't know what—ate out that little mouse's heart. Gruesome!

"Oh, something a little more cheerful: You wouldn't think that mouse trapping could lead to romance, but it did for me once. A mouse made himself the room-mate of a young lady. She couldn't get rid of it. But *I* did. You can't imagine how she thanked me....

"How did I get in the mouse-trapping business, I suppose you want to ask me? Well, there was one thing that happened that set me to it.

"I had an old car once that I didn't drive much. If I wanted to go somewheres, I generally took my truck. My car just sat stored in the garage on the farm.

"One day I thought, 'It ain't good for that car to just sit there wasting away. I should give it a good run on the road.'

"So I decided to drive the car to town to stock up on groceries. I usually take my truck, but this time I took my old car.

"The car drove pretty good for an old car. That's why I keep it.

"Anyway, I drove right up to the front of the grocery and walked past the car. What did I see? About a half-dozen mice came spilling out from under the hood and running in all directions!

"A lady coming out of the grocery threw her hands up, dropped her bag, and let out the most godawful scream.

"'What the hell!' I said,—although I don't usually cuss in front of ladies.

"I opened the hood of the car and there was a nest made by those mice. A nest right on top of the engine, almost filling up the whole engine compartment. A mouse nest of dry grass, brown leaves, shredded cardboard, twigs, and such.

"Those mice could've burned up my car and maybe me in it!

"Oh, they must've got a little toasted while the car was running! No wonder they hotfooted it out of the car when I stopped.

"I tell you I was so mad I could have bit off and spit out the heads of all them mice that might have burned up my car and me in it.

"So, that was why I got into mouse trapping in a

big way. Not to break my arm patting myself on the back, but nobody does it better than me. . .

"Now, all this talk of killing doesn't mean I glory in it. I'm not tenderhearted, but, still, there is something pitiful in the mouse-catching, mouse-killing, business.

"For example. I once heard a mouse scratching away in a drawer at night. The next day, I set my trap in the back of the drawer. Of course, I caught her. In cleaning out the drawer, I found under a baseball cap a nest of shredded paper and, among the shreds, six pink naked baby mice waiting for their mother's milk. When I uncovered them, they wriggled about in their blind helplessness. Poor things, orphans now. What could I do? I took them outside and exposed them in the woods.

"I know a lot about mouse-killing. I've done a lot of it, but that doesn't mean I like it. It's just something that's got to be done."

\* \* \* \* \*

My cabin in the woods is actually a 46' x 10' mobile home to which a 15' x 11' wood frame room was added.

The aluminum siding of the mobile home did not present a suitable bosky look, so the builders of the new room sided its exterior with rustic cedar. The result is a disjointed combination somewhat held together by a shingled roof over the two components. Anyway, a cabin is to be lived in, not looked at to be admired as architecture.

The cedar siding and the wide overhanging roof eaves of the addition turned out to be a welcoming invitation to bats, who can cling easily to the rough cedar—(the smooth aluminum offers no clawhold)—, finding shelter from the elements under the eaves. The cabin went unoccupied for several years; it may have been then that the bats took over squattership undisturbed.

The bats have never gotten into the cabin itself, nor are they roosting on the building during the day. They just alight throughout the night to rest a bit, or, as I see in the evidence of moth wings along the walls, enjoy a meal,—not a sit-down meal, but a hang-down one.

– – –(A matter of organic crudity: I used to wonder how bats could urinate and defecate while hanging upside down without making a revolting mess of themselves. In fact, they do no such thing; they right themselves to do it right.)– – –

Even if the bats have not taken up cohabitation inside with me, they are an imposition and a hygienic nuisance. I have to clean their droppings from the walls, the windows and sills. Their poop right at my front door is a deterrent to visitors who shudder at the very thought of bats. (One of my field guides has a remark that what separates the true naturalist from the dilettante are spiders, snakes, and bats. The bat is certainly the least cuddly of those 75 species of mammals that live in Minnesota.)

In battling bats, I considered how I might rid my cabin of them without resorting to murder. I had heard of owl statues that are put out to scare off varmints. I bought one and mounted it on a board projecting from the outside wall facing the bats' favorite haunting corner. A menacing owl now on the scene, the bats will flee for their lives.

The bats were not fooled by the plastic predator. As I discovered in all the droppings on the sill the next morning, I might as well have set up a manikin of Count Dracula.

Last night after dark, heavy rains began to roll in. I went outside with a flashlight to see whether the bats were taking refuge from the weather.

Sure enough, right by the front door, under the eaves at the inner corner of the junction between mobile home and added room, a bat snuggled.

A flat, squarish gob of fur hanging upside down, a claw on a wing showing to one side. It was a brown bat or a little brown bat, (the only difference being whether more or less than the 1/2" length differential between the species).

I went back inside, not for a ruler but for a fishing rod. I took it out to the deck, extended the tip of the rod to the wall next to the bat and flicked my wrist, scraping the bat from the wall and launching him out into the downpour.

With flashlight in one hand and fishing rod in the other, I made my way around the cedar-wall portion of the cabin, serving eviction on a half-dozen bats. It may be that one I drove off from the front immediately alighted on the back, from which I drove him off again.

The owl gave me a brief fright, when the beam of my flashlight briefly crossed its reflective yellow eyes.

Whether my harassment will be effective remains to be seen.

I know that bats have their place in the natural scheme-of-things, they do us humans a favor by eating mosquitoes, and they are being decimated by white-nose syndrome. Nonetheless, I feel no personal duty of hospitality toward them.

I wonder... If I suspend a big rubber snake from the eaves...

\* \* \* \* \*

Here I am in the north woods, the wild land of wolves and bears and even a reputed mountain lion. Yet, I am snug, safe and secure in my cabin.

Meanwhile, I receive a phone call from Janet back at home in suburbia, where Nature is supposed to be fully subdued. "Help!" she pleads. "The raccoons are trying to break into our attic!"

\* \* \* \* \*

560 miles away from home, I cannot rush to Janet's quick rescue. She'll have to use her female wiliness to fend off the raccoons.

When I am on the home scene, however, I can be effective in dealing with a breaking-and-entering by unwelcome critters.

The previous owners of our house found the kitchen too narrow for a sit-down meal, so they cut open the outside wall and built an alcove to serve as a breakfast nook for a small table and two chairs.

Instead of laying a concrete foundation, however, they just laid the wall sill on the dirt and built the alcove.

One day, I happened to be out in the side yard and saw a large hole dug under the sill and into the alcove. Uh-oh, a home invasion! What had done it,—a rabbit, a woodchuck, a raccoon?

I presumed that the critter was inside. Fetching a flashlight and a brass school hand bell (to frighten the critter out), I climbed down into the crawl space.

Removing a small wooden panel between the main house crawl space and the alcove, I shone the flashlight into the dark of the space under the floor of our breakfast nook.

I saw a moving back-and-forth, a black-and-white stripe. Skunk!

I would certainly not ring the bell now, frightening the skunk to discharge its defense. I quietly replaced the wood panel and withdrew from the crawl space.

How could I evict that skunk without him repelling me or fumigating the breakfast nook from below?

I had heard of a man in similar situation who decided to *fight fire with fire*, in his case gas attack with gas attack. Attempting to drive out a skunk from under his porch, he tossed in a stink bomb, but only succeeded in burning down his house; (no skunk carcass was to be found in the ashes).

Well now, I thought, if Nature Norm can't deal with the problem, who can?

I knew that the skunk is a nocturnal creature. He's got to eat and he will go foraging at night. Therefore, I would not attempt to confront him and drive him out. Instead, I would let him go out and then prevent his getting back in.

I laid aside a supply of bricks I would use to seal the hole after the skunk had gone out.

The floor of the alcove was dirt, so wouldn't that skunk's feet likely be dirty?

That afternoon I laid a sheet of white paper outside the hole.

That night I stayed up until 3 a.m., a time that I figured the skunk to be out-and-about. Taking up flashlight again, I returned to the hole. Sure enough, there on that sheet of paper were skunk dirty footprints laid down in the direction of exiting. I picked up the paper and shoved the bricks into the hole to block reentry.

After a good night's sleep and a breakfast without worry of a stink from below the floor, I returned to a do a more thorough blockage and also added a row of imbedded bricks to the outside perimeter of the alcove.

Problem solved! Householder security restored.

* * * * *

The timberjay well deserves its nickname, *camp robber*.

My partner was new to the north woods, but he was settling in well. We had found a pleasant campsite. It was about time for lunch.

I was standing facing him from the opposite side of the campfire circle and saw it all.

My partner took up a jar of peanut butter, a jar of jelly, a loaf of bread, and a knife. He laid the two jars and the bread on a big log and sat down next to them to make a sandwich.

He took out a slice of bread, slathered it with peanut butter, and laid it on the log next to him on his right side.

A timberjay swept in from behind him, snatched up the peanut buttered bread, and flew off.

My partner didn't see what happened, because his head was facing left and down as he resealed the peanut butter jar, opened the jelly jar, and drew another slice of bread from the loaf.

When he finished jellying the slice, he turned back to the right to complete the assembly of his peanut-butter-and-jelly sandwich.

He made a little start of surprise.

He looked down on the ground in front of him, then got up and searched the end of the log and the back of the log.

"How did you do that?" he demanded. (He suspected one of my pranks.)

"Do what?"

"Take the half of my sandwich."

"I didn't take it. A camp robber did."

"Who?"

"Not *Who*? *What*. A camp robber is a bird. It was a timberjay, alias Canada jay, alias gray jay."

"You mean a little bird took my half-sandwich?"

"A timberjay is not a little bird."

My partner scanned the treetops skeptically. He gave a grunt of frustration.

He sat back down, put the loaf of bread protectively on the ground between his ankles, drew out a slice of bread and proceeded to cover it with peanut butter. The jellied slice was in his lap, and he hunched over it in defense.

All the while that he was re-peanut buttering, he was searching the trees in apprehension. Because of that, he had peanut buttered his thumb, which he now licked off.

He slapped the two pieces of bread together and stood up.

Clutching his peanut-butter-and-jelly sandwich in both hands, staring into the trees around him, he shouted in defiance, "Come on, camp robber! See if you can take it from me now!"

The timberjay is a sneak thief. It lurks at campsites and will hit-and-fly, stealing whatever strikes its fancy, especially food of such kinds not usually available in the northwoods environment.

In the territory of the timberjay, you'd better not lay your ring down in the open when you are washing up.

You might think that in the woods you're getting away from it all, but, even there, it's a wicked, wicked world.

\* \* \* \* \*

The chipmunk scampered along the top of the log. (*Scamper* is the verb that always goes with chipmunks.)

I immediately began a persistent "Tchk-Tchk-Tchk," a sound made by flicking the tip of the tongue against the upper teeth and sucking spit.

"Tchk-Tchk-Tchk-Tchk."

The chipmunk descended from the log. I could see the little striped brown of his body and tail cut a swath through the overhanging vegetation toward me.

"Tchk-Tchk-Tchk-Tchk."

The chipmunk emerged onto the road, where I stood. He came straight to me, until he was between the toes of my two feet.

As I continued my summoning call, he rose on his hind legs and looked up at me, a tower over his little body.

He sized me up.

His quizzical expression was as if to say, "Who

and what are you? You seem to be speaking my language or the language of cousin squirrel, but I can't understand a word of it."

Now, this was no urban park chipmunk used to coming to humans to beg a handout. He was a fully wild Minnesota woods chipmunk. Yet, he responded to my attempt at interspecies communication.

However, as he found what I had to say unintelligible, I held his interest for just a few seconds. He fell back to all fours, turned away, crossed the road and continued his foraging.

Well, I had at least provided the chipmunk a novel experience out of the ordinariness of his usual day.

* * * * *

I was standing on the edge of the deck, arms folded, quietly observing the birds flitting among the trees on an overcast morning, when a furry brown body came charging straight toward me.

Big eyes saw me looming above—a fright in those eyes—, then the brown body veered aside and dashed to disappearance under my cabin.

The fright was mutual, for, in the few seconds of the encounter, I didn't at first recognize what was apparently in full attack charge against me.

But it was not an attack against, only an apparent flight from. Just a rabbit; no threat to me at all.

The rabbit had run toward me with such directness and speed that I didn't believe it was just a high-spirited frolic of animal energy. More likely a desperate run-for-your-life.

I looked in the direction from which the rabbit had come, but I did not perceive anything pursuing....

This has been my interpretation of the rabbit's behavior: Fearful flight, of course no attack against me at all,—up to the point where the rabbit saw me suddenly looming above. What happened at that instant needs no interpretive conjecturing. The instinct of self-preservation activated, and the rabbit veered off away from me.

The rabbit did not stop in front of me, look up and wonder, "Is this human out to get me, or is he just standing around innocently without any predatory intent toward me? Or might he even protect me from what's after me? Hmm... What should I do? Run away, run to him, or stay here and think about it some more...?"

No. The rabbit's flight from me was instantaneous. In the matter of survival, mulling over choices might be fatal. Run, then! The instinct of self-preservation must have timely application for it to be effective in its purpose.

As for myself, when the furry brown body was in what seemed full attack against me, I stiffened in a fright of my own. Startled, I stood dumb and paralyzed, the instinct in me failing to activate. The perceived, or misperceived, attack charge lasted at most two or three seconds, I say in defense of my instinct. Yet, such a brief stupefaction might be fatal to a rabbit.

It was only after the animal had veered off and

disappeared under my cabin that I interpreted what had happened. "Just a rabbit."

It is not that we humans have lost our instinct of self-preservation. It is just that we are so much in our own attack mode, complacent in our dominance of Nature, that the self-protective, self-preservational instinctual reaction may be slow to kick in.

The plodding mechanism of thinking, of judgment, overrides organic instinct. I may even conjure up in my mind all kinds of purely imaginary threats and dangers and be on anxious guard against them; the rabbit, meanwhile, faces real threats, but does not, I don't believe, live a life of constant anxieties.

A sudden encounter between a wild animal and a human produces mutual shock. The fight-or-flight alternatives then confront each one. If the animal attacks, it may kill a human in the skirmish, but it is the human mind and will, not any instinct, that will assure total victory of the human in any interspecies war.

The rabbit, defenseless, ought to flee from the human in every encounter. The rabbit is on the human hunter's slaughter list.

\* \* \* \* \*

I was standing on the slope of the Point, when I detected a soft swimming close to the shore behind me.

I turned around and advanced to see what it might be.

A mink emerged from the water and climbed to the top of a boulder.

Seeing me, the mink stopped and tensed. She fixed on me with a ferocious glare.

I was not that close to her, didn't think that I was crowding her or posing a threat just by standing where I was. Yet, from her tense stance and hard stare, I got the feeling that she was going to attack me, never mind the huge differences in our respective size and weight.

I felt a fleeting fear, perhaps absurd in a confrontation with such a small animal. I braced myself and held out my fishing rod as my only defensive weapon.

There were a few seconds of mutual suspense, the mink facing the fight-or-flight alternatives.

Then the mink turned away, scurried down the shoreline boulders, and disappeared into a crevice.

She must have had young there. That was why she had shown defensive ferocity, even against an animal multiples of her size.

My own tension eased, now that the mink was gone from my sight.

Needless to say, I did not stick a snooping nose into the crevice the mink had entered.

What is a true danger, a threat to life, and what is just a harmless but momentarily frightening chance encounter?

The mink's maternal defensiveness was not put

into action by an attack upon me. Instead, the nurturance instinct overrode, as she retreated to check on, and extend care to, her kits.

If she had attacked me, and, say, I had killed her, her kits would have been orphaned. They would surely then perish. So, her retreat saved them.

It also saved me what could have been a nasty skirmish with a little hellion....

Some long time later, also on the peninsula of the Point, I almost stepped upon a small black furry bulk. I bent down to examine it.

A fresh-killed mink. It took me a bit to identify it, because the mink was decapitated, its severed head so gnawed that, featureless, it looked like a furry egg. The forelimbs were mangled, but the rest of the body was untouched. This was no kill-to-eat; this was a kill-to-kill. The mink, a creature ferocious itself, had become the victim of a more ferocious ferocity.

* * * * *

On the tip of the Point, gazing out at the lake...

Just below me, to my right, a muskrat came down the rock and entered the water.

He swam out on the surface, his big hind feet paddling, his long tail waving back and forth in slicing undulations.

He then dove.

A series of big bubbles blooped up in three places.

The muskrat bobbed to the surface, strands of pale green aquatic vegetation that he had uprooted now gripped crosswise in his jaws.

He paddled back toward me and came ashore on a small ledge just four feet from where I stood. He took no more notice of me than if I were a tree,—(perhaps a recommendation for a northwoods naturalist to dress all in brown, as I happened to be).

The muskrat turned his back to me and began to consume his breakfast salad.

I took the opportunity of nearness to inspect the muskrat's coat, but not with a furrier's eye. His pelage (not pelt) looked well-suited to aquatic immersion. As soon as the muskrat got out of the water, the fur on the back, standing up in bristles, became instantly dry. The dark hairs on the lower body clung close but would need just a bit of grooming to dry out and fluff. There was a small bare spot just above the tail.

Oh, and the muskrat's feet were very ugly.

As I watched the muskrat, I was struck by how his mannerisms and appearance affiliated him in kinship with other mammals. Before he began to eat, he wiped his face with two forepaws, as a cat washes itself. Feeling an itch, he scratched it with a hind foot, as a dog does. He hunched his backside into a ball against the chill breeze,—a rabbit cold-weather posture. Then, too, he handled his food with forepaws, as does the squirrel. In his triangular head and pointed snout, I saw a rat or shrew. His profile reminded me of a woodchuck. And his general form was definitely beaverlike.

– – –(One day at the camp, some children came running to me. "Nature Norm, Nature Norm!" they exclaimed excitedly, "There's a beaver in the swimming area! Come see!"

I followed them down to the lake.

"No, that's not a beaver. It's only a muskrat," I told the children.

(I shouldn't have used the word *only*. In Nature there is no *only*.)– –

The muskrat on the Point finished his first course, then went out in the lake for a second helping.

Once again, the surface swim, the dive, the big bubbles, the re-emergence on the surface with a mouthful, and the return to the same small ledge for the backside-to-me feeding.

The muskrat next swam around the Point to another ledge barely out of the water. Some strands of tender aquatic greens lay there, whether put previously by the muskrat or carried in by the waves. The muskrat picked those up and chomped away.

The hungry fellow then went out for yet another foraging dive.

Food was nearby and plentiful, for Pelican is a weedy lake, underwater Eden to a muskrat.

As he paddled back to his first dining spot, the muskrat definitely saw me with those little black beady blinking eyes, but once again he paid me no mind.

He stepped onto the ledge, turned his furry hunched back to me, and resumed the satisfaction of an apparently robust appetite. His palate was discriminating, in that he preferred the white roots to the pale green shoots.

From the corner of my eye, I detected a moving V wake on the surface of the cove to my left. Another muskrat swimming along.

The second muskrat seemed headed elsewhere, but he abruptly veered toward the Point. He came ashore, as disregarding of me as the first muskrat was.

I wondered what kind of muskrat encounter would ensue. As among us humans, among animals it may be Love or Strife.

The second muskrat ambled around the tip of the Point.

When the first muskrat saw him, he immediately took to the water and skedaddled toward the middle of the lake, unexpected to me, because the intruder was smaller than the first muskrat and so not particularly threatening. Some neighbor incompatibility, I suppose.

The intruder glided into the water and swam on close to the shore.

At that, the first muskrat swam back from the open water and paddled along the shore in the same direction the intruder had taken. He disappeared from view among the boulders on the shoreline. Some confrontation ahead?

\* \* \* \* \*

I was paddling along the shoreline of Myrtle Lake, when the shoreline suddenly erupted, as if a glacial boulder had launched itself into the lake.

Out of the corner of my eye I saw that the big ploosh was not made by an inert stone, but rather by a very alive 50-pound beaver.

It is unusual to see a beaver out-and-about at midday, for the beaver is generally active at dawn, at dusk, and in dark. Further unusual, this beaver was unsheltered. It had been exposed, resting on a flat stone in front of the shoreline tall grasses.

The beaver is a homebody. In fact, a homemaker, if you take that word to describe one who makes his own home, then make himself at home in it.

The beaver, a do-it-all handyman, obtains the building materials, transports them to the chosen home site, erects the structure, provides an exclusive access by means of an underwater entryway, and furnishes the home with enough food to see through any long northwoods winter. The self-sufficient beaver is logger, teamster, architect, builder, carpenter, craftsman, mud-mason, and provisioner all-in-one. And then, of course, homeowner.

A beaver generally chooses a shoreline site for his home; he can then get his woody groceries nearby. If the body of water is a shallow pond surrounded by marsh, however, he may build his domed home right in the middle, just like the northwoods vacationer who buys a cabin on an island, where he can survey the full 360° panorama of his water domain.

The beaver is a very familial animal. That built home—(suitably called a *lodge*, given its woodsy setting)—will be occupied by the beaver nuclear family, —the parents and their offspring. As soon as the young ones are able, they are recruited into apprenticeship in the family enterprise, helping out with home maintenance and repairs, thereby learning the skills of the construction trade that they too will follow when they grow up.

I found no beaver lodge on Myrtle Lake, so this particular beaver may have been out prospecting possibilities for a new home site.

Outside of their own family, beavers are not sociable with their kind, and there comes a time when the young ones must be driven out to make home space for a new batch of offspring. And so, the beavers get dispersed across the waterscape.

The beaver is territorial, inhospitable, and quick to rile at any intrusion, whether by other beavers or trespassing humans.

Northland fishermen and beavers necessarily come into contact, for they frequent the same medium. The fisherman intends no molestation of the beaver, but, for his part, the beaver carries his possessive territoriality to hostility. Inadvertently crowd a beaver, and he will issue a "Scram!" order by smacking his broad tail upon the surface of the water. The effect is like a shotgun blast. The first time that happened to me—from an unseen beaver close behind me—I nearly jumped out of the canoe in fright.

I recently heard about an incident in which a beaver knocked a woman off her standup paddleboard and began to chew on her leg (which was flesh, not wood). The woman's frantic thrashing and screams drew a nearby boater to her rescue. He beat back the beaver with an oar, pulled the woman from the water, and took her to the hospital for sutures of her wounds. The beaver's only excuse for such unprovoked attack was that it was rabid. (It was later captured and killed to prevent any further assaults.)

I lifted my paddle from the water and paused in my course, waiting for the beaver to rise up from his plunge off the Myrtle Lake shoreline. He did come up for air and swam along. I then paddled parallel with him, not close but apparently enough to irritate him. He finally whacked the water with his tail and dove.

This beaver was typically cantankerous, but not, I don't think, psychopathic.

After his parting shot, I withdrew out to the open lake.

The beaver then swam along the shoreline back and forth a bit aimlessly, until he returned to the same flat rock I had driven him from.

"Damn human nuisance!" he may have thought of me.

\* \* \* \* \*

Out in the middle of the lake, three otters popped up their heads like periscopes, pivoted in unison to spot me in my canoe, then, judging my canoe too buoyant to be sinkable and me too big to be edible, they submerged to resume their predations underwater.

Not a Nazi submarine wolf pack. A Minnesota Pelican Lake otter pack....

A few days later, I was canoeing close along the shore of Susan Bay, gliding through duckweed and over lily pads.

From behind me two otters suddenly appeared, swimming swiftly one behind the other.

On impulse I paddled after them.

The water there was too shallow for an otter's deep-water escape dive.

When I drew close, I saw that the second otter was a young one following her mother.

The little one cried out an alarm. She couldn't keep up with her mother. She had the natatorial aptitude, but she lacked the power and stamina. Now I-in-the-canoe, a floating monster, pressed from behind. The little otter's *squeak-squeak-squeak* meant "Help!".

The mother heard her, swung around, and raised her head and torso out of the water to assess the situation. She then waited for her little one to catch up.

I quit paddling my pursuit and sat quietly on a patch of pads.

The little one joined her mother and, reassured, stopped her alarm squeaks. The two of them then continued ahead along the shoreline in the same single file, the little one hurrying behind.

I did not paddle forward until they were fully gone.

The wild shouldn't be pressed too close. We humans must check the aggressive instinct that seems to come so natural to us. We must back off. The wild is ever-other and should remain so.

* * * * *

The missing Minnesota animal is the moose. Moose numbers have declined so much that the state Department of Natural Resources asked people to report moose sightings. (A moose is a big animal, and, if there, is easily seen.) When, however, the public responded by reporting more moose than expected, the DNR ungratefully rejected the sightings, claiming that some people were reporting the same moose twice or different people were reporting the same moose, in short, seeing double or counting one as many. (By such reasoning, there might be only one moose in the whole state of Minnesota, that one an exhibitionist.)

It's been some years since I myself saw a moose in Minnesota. (That wouldn't prevent me from suffering a moose hallucination and reporting that as real to the DNR.) The last moose I saw was a big bull that had set up a roadblock of Ely.

While canoeing, portaging, and camping on Isle Royale National Park, however, my partner and I encountered moose as common as squirrels. I would have needed a tally counter there. We saw the moose especially in marshes and bogs along portage routes.

One night there, as I lay in my sleeping bag, I heard the heavy hooves of a moose stepping on the rock just outside the tent. The moose was so close that I had been awakened by his deep breathing and chomping on the vegetation. Moose are notoriously poor sighted and clumsy besides. I was afraid that the lumbering oaf might inadvertently step on my head, which was the part of me next to the tent wall that the moose was muscling against.

I was in a dilemma as to whether to shout to drive the moose off—(but what if, startled, he trampled the tent?)—or to whisper a warning to my sleeping tent mate—(but then, what was he supposed to do?). In the end, I stayed silent, all tense, listening intently and clutching the hem of my sleeping bag. At last, the moose huffed and munched away from the tent. I awoke the next morning, head still attached, body uncrushed, as did my partner. When I told him about my scare, he shrugged it off as a moose mirage in a dream.

A friend of mine once shot a moose. He invited me over for a moose dinner. I was interested in the novelty of moose-on-a-plate, so I accepted. The moose meat was...different. The next night, my friend invited me for more moose, but I was reluctant; once was enough. "But I've got a freezer full of moose. Please help me eat it!" my friend pleaded. "I need some space for ice cream." Which goes to show that eating a moose is a greater challenge than shooting one.

Moose frequent lowlands, marshes, sluggish creeks, and bogs, where they can find substantial amounts of the aquatic vegetation they favor as food. My particular section of Pelican Lake doesn't offer much of that, and, besides, there are too many people and too much goings-on to be tolerable to such an antisocial beast as the moose.

The male moose possesses that combination of worst human traits: He is stupid and ornery. When in rut, he may run you down as a misperceived rival or ram your car for spite.

I'd like to sight a Minnesota moose, there on some distant shoreline, he up to his bulging waist in the water, chewing waterweeds, long strands of which hang dripping from his massive antlers. A picturesque northland view, but a very long view, seen from the safe detachment of my canoe in the middle of the lake.

The decline of the moose has been variously attributed to global warming—(moose do not endure heat well)—, a brain parasite or liver fluke from deer, winter tick infestation, various bacterial infections, predation of moose calves by the resurgent wolf population, overhunting, or habitat loss.

If the Minnesota moose does truly go missing, it will at least survive in the imagery and symbolism of the North. A symbol will not step on your head or run you down.

\* \* \* \* \*

The howling of wolves in the middle of the night.

I wake up. I am neither startled nor frightened, but, rather, attuned, as if responding to a call.

The wolves sound far away. In a different sense, I am far away from them, snug under a comforter, lying on a plush mattress, secure under a hard roof and within enclosing walls with shut door.

We are separate and far away from one another, the wolves and I.

Our only connection is their howling and my alert, wide-awake, concentrated listening.

* * * * *

I have had some up-close encounters with bears.

The confrontations go back all the way to my infancy.

My mother told me that my aunt bought a teddy bear to be my crib companion. When my mother tried to lay the bear next to me in the crib, however, I took such fright that I screamed bloody murder. My mother withdrew the bear. When she tried again the next day, I reacted the same way.

My mother had no wish to terrorize me, but she wanted to show my aunt gratitude for the gift by a photo of me cuddling the bear. My mother decided to wait a month or so, by which time I may have increased in strength and acquired some bravery to accept the bear.

That month later, my mother waited until I was asleep and then slipped the bear into the crib at my side.

When my mother returned the next morning, she found me awake with a look of triumph on my flushed face. The bedcovers were all in disarray, as if after a great struggle. As for the bear, it had had its right arm torn off. Its face was gnawed and matted with spit. The bear's left ear was ripped open. The tiny round bell that had been in that ear was missing.

The next day I tinkled.

I can verify my mother's story, because I still have that teddy bear. Its right arm has been re-attached with carpet thread. The right ear is plump with its little bell' inside, but the left ear, flat and limp, is empty....

In adulthood, my encounters have been with black bears.

Bears and other large animals of the woods commonly avail themselves of human-made open passages, like logging roads and portage trails.

On Minnesota-Ontario Boundary Waters trips, I would be walking a portage trail, the canoe on my shoulders, when, turning a curve, I would come upon a bear and he upon me.

The suddenness of the encounter, without a formal introduction or even a gradual coming-into-view, would unnerve both the bear and myself.

The bear would dash off in fright, whether back down the trail or into the brush, breaking branches and bouncing off trees. As for me, I would stagger back, attempt a turnabout, stumble, and usually wind up sprawled, crushed by the canoe on top of me.

A party of us *voyageurs* had just set up camp below Rebecca Falls in Quetico Provincial Park. We were to eat mostly freeze-dried rations for the week, but the outfitter had provided us with steaks for the first night. As the steaks grilled away, a light breeze off the lake wafted the odors up into the woods behind us. I happened to glance into the woods, and there, downwind, was a large black bear standing leaning against a tree sniffing. The members of our party took turns on watch through the night. The next day, we abandoned the campsite and paddled far away from sure trouble.

Another time, I was guiding a group of teenage boys through the Boundary Waters. We had tents pitched and camp set up for the week ahead. It was lunchtime.

"Don't throw the apple cores into the woods," I told the boys. "Bears love apples. Throw the cores in the fire pit, and we'll burn them up tonight."

The boys did as they were told.

Just a few minutes later, I turned to see a black bear at the fire pit, his head down in it, eating the apple cores. That bear had walked in amidst eight people in broad daylight.

I gathered up all the aluminum pots and pans and led the boys in an orchestra of cacophonous banging with spoons, until the bear ambled off, irritated but not intimidated.

"Break camp. We're moving," I ordered the group.

"But I just got my tent pitched in the perfect spot," one boy protested.

"No matter," I told him. "The bear has found us, and he'll be back."

And so, to our immediate inconvenience but long-term security, we broke camp and paddled off to a small island, a site not bear-proof but likely bear-free.

In all my trips to the Boundary Waters, I never lost a food pack to a bear. My rope-and-pulley suspension of the food from a high tree branch was effective.

Over the years, the black bear has become less and less fearful of the human. There have even been reported unprovoked attacks and maulings, something I would never have expected in the behavior of the black bear.

When in the woods, I never want to run into a bear, but there is near Orr an opportunity to meet bears under circumstances without troublous involvement. To which I now guide the reader....

# Excursions

About twenty miles from my cabin is a black bear *sanctuary*, where bears are fed daily, which feeding is on exhibit, the tourists watching from an elevated boardwalk.

"Do not feed the bears" is a common prohibition of the national parks of the West, but, in the sanctuary, the bears are fed. They are served piles of fruit-and-nut trail mix and peanuts in the shell. The all-you-can-eat buffet is spread about on split log troughs and flat boulders in the grassy lowland below the boardwalk.

The founder of the sanctuary was a logger who used to shoot nuisance bears, until, after a conversion to sympathy, he decided to feed them instead.

One of the members of the sanctuary board is a bear-hunting guide,—a paradox until you consider that the bear he feeds today will be the bear a client of his shoots tomorrow. A local told me that the guides set up their own feeding stations around the perimeter of the sanctuary to bait bears for killing. In 2016, hunters in Minnesota *harvested* (their word, sounds better than *slaughtered)* 2,641 bears.

The members of Trout Unlimited or Ducks Unlimited show dedicated concern for creatures only out of their own respective self-interest. A trout fisherman needs fish to catch, a hunter ducks to shoot. The lives of fish and fowl must be nurtured, in order for them to be taken. Some conservationists wish to preserve,—for their own consumption. It's just a matter of stocking the meat locker.

(I don't know how that motive can apply to bear hunting.)

Janet and I spent an evening at the black bear sanctuary. About forty bears accepted the invitation to supper.

There was a gender segregation, the males to one side, the females with cubs to the other, something like the contemporary American family.

When we first arrived at the top of the observation boardwalk, we faced three cubs up in an elm tree, as their mothers gorged below them. The cubs needed no arboreal refuge from us harmless human spectator tourists. Awkwardly clutching the trunk or pressed into a crotch, they looked uncomfortable.

I adjudged most of the bears as obese, but then, this being late August, they are fattening up for the coming winter hibernation. Some had bellies almost dragging the ground; their general form was porcine. They were not only well-fed, they were stuffed, as, after the hunt, they might be again.

Quite strange, the volunteer docents at the sanctuary were all from Britain. No bears or bear baiting in overcivilized Great Britain anymore; not much of the wild left over there. One volunteer told me that even their native red squirrels had gone extinct, displaced and done in by imported North American gray squirrels,—the British victims of imperialistic colonialism for once.

A lady, slim and lovely, walked among the bears, replenishing the food piles at the stations. She was a principal of the sanctuary, the expert, the one who knows all the assembled bears by name. (The by-name rather than by-number indicates a personal relatedness.) She was very blonde, a Goldilocks with so many more than just the Three Bears.

Janet and I returned to the cabin in the dark. As we turned into the access road, Janet said she saw a moving black bulk ahead. Our own neighbor bear or just an after-image?

\* \* \* \* \*

The gale winds of the past several days now subsided, the air warm, the water calm, conditions on this early morning beckoned me to some canoeing.

I launched my canoe and set out.

A mermaid was sitting on the Point, half-in, half-out of the water. She gazed out contemplatively, in solitary admiration of the beauty of Pelican Lake.

I was reluctant to disturb her reverie, but I had to paddle past her to get into Susan Bay, so my intrusion was necessary.

"Good morning, lovely!" I saluted her.

"Oh, hello!" she greeted me, taking me not as intruder, but recognizing me as a familiar component of the local color and scene.

"And what will you be up to today?" I asked her as I paddled past.

"My dad is going to take me out on the lake swimming in a little while," she told me.

A very suitable activity for a mermaid, I thought to myself.

I paddled on, leaving the mermaid to her appreciation and attunement.

I drew up behind Hahne Island, which was still in some comfortable shade. I caught a chunky largemouth bass there, his belly swollen with recent meals to which he tried to add my shad-imitating spinner-jig. I rebuked him for his foolishness in trying to eat the inedible, then eased him back into the water.

I next put a floating prop-bait on my line, cast it out, and chugged it in short jerks. Very convincing simulation of a frog, because a kingfisher dove to an attack, raising a splash. The kingfisher flew off empty beaked, expressing her frustration by a scolding rattle. I laid my rod aside. What, would I next reel in an eagle?

I proceeded amidst and among the pelicans, some on the rock islets, some afloat. As I paddled along silently, they didn't react to me as any threat. Still, they wanted a certain distance maintained between us. Some stepped into the water off the far side of an islet; those afloat paddled steadily away.

A pontoon boat from the resort steamed directly toward the largest of the pelican islets. Why can't you keep your distance?, I complained to those who could not hear my thoughts.

The pontoon boat headed straight into the islet. I then saw one of the passengers dump a bucketload of fish offal from the resort's fish cleaning shed upon the rock pile, then another bucketload.

The pelicans had all abandoned their islet at the approach of the boat, but now, at its backing-up, they returned, racing the gulls to feed on the disposal. Other pelicans that had seen what happened flew over from here and there on Susan Bay.

Are we turning the pelicans into scrap-pickers, like the gulls, already long corrupted? Is the presence of the pelicans on Pelican Lake due, not so much to the live fish in the water here, as to the fish-filth dumped daily upon the rock?

And I myself here on Pelican Lake, fishing for Nature. Will I catch the living fish, or are there only scraps of offal for me to pick through?

I left the demoralizing scene behind and paddled down the west shoreline of Susan Bay.

I went into each little cove. Very shallow water,— too shallow for the fish now, but the frogs kronked out their contentment there.

These northern Minnesota lakes are on rock and surrounded by rock. Some of the shoreline is haphazard heaps of glaciated boulders or sheer rock walls or rock points and promontories. The canoeist finds his attention drawn as much to the projections and elevations of rock as to the surface of water.

I paddled my canoe to the shore, got out, and pulled my canoe up, bow and stern, in precarious balance on two flattish stones. I then stepped onto the solidity.

I disembarked there with the idea of ascending the hill near State Rock for an overlook upon the lake.

Clambering up the slope and through scattered brush, I looked for the highest perspective. The sun heating the rock made the air above it hot and dry. I found myself taking deeper breaths, and my heart beat stronger for the exertion.

Among the expected ground-hugging junipers and the vertically assertive great pines, I was surprised to find oak trees, seemingly out of place in the conifer woods. They didn't feel themselves out-of-place, for they enjoyed the fellowship of numbers there.

I was pleased to also discover ripe blueberries among the junipers. Not come for harvesting, I had no cup or bowl, so I just ate on the spot. The fullest of the flavor is attained by throwing a handful into the mouth, rather than just eating one blueberry at a time. The blueberries were warm from the sun, but I did not like them the less for that; I could not begrudge the agent and cause of their ripening.

Someone once asked me how to identify the wild blueberry plant. "By the blueberries on it," I answered. What we most value in Nature is use.

I found the jawbone of a northern pike, some spiny teeth still in it. I doubt the fish was a rock-climber. An eagle or osprey had dined on a dry rock table.

The constant of the woods is the trees, of course. (Insects too seem to be a constant. I pulled off an oak branchlet to use as a switch against the deerflies.) As for the large animals, they seem not to be there...and suddenly they are.

As I stood upon a high bare slope, a fawn suddenly appeared, bounding up toward me from below. He or she stopped abruptly and looked up at me, perhaps the first human being the fawn had seen in its young life. (I was on the state forest land, where there is neither resort nor cabin.)

The fawn regarded me for a half-minute or so, I staying still and casting a benevolent glance down upon the dear little deer.

The fawn tiptoed along beside me, then stopped again to look upon the phenomenon of my existence.

I slowly pivoted to return the recognition of another creature.

I did not reach out, nor did the fawn seek my touch. I am only Nature Norm, not Orpheus or St. Francis of Assisi; the fawn was no character in a Disney cartoon. Even so, creaturely fellow-feeling flowed between us.

The fawn stepped along behind me, not in any great hurry or flight. Peeking through the brush, I could still see the dappled fur and white flag tail.

At last, the fawn descended through the brush out of sight. I thought I heard a faint cough from another direction, the dam calling back her wayward offspring.

Now I was on the highest belvedere, from which I could see much of the lake through the trees on the hillside. I myself was at the level of the treetops on the horizon at the far end of the lake. I experienced the lake from high above the lake, as is possible on the masses of the so-called Precambrian rocks of the Canadian Shield.

I then felt a fleeting apprehension that the waves cast up by the motorboats passing below might dislodge my canoe from its perch, set it adrift and leave me stranded.

I descended to see the waves just slip under my canoe on its platform without rocking or even touching the canoe.

This magnificent lake. I had been down upon it, afloat, then high above it in the air but on solid rock, multidimensional positioning and perspective.

As I paddled homeward past the Point, the mermaid was no longer there. I expect that she was immersed, as, in a different sense, I too was.

\* \* \* \* \*

Swan Creek empties into Pelican Lake just beyond State Rock. The creek comes out of Swan Lake. Whether that name derives from the trumpeter or Tchaikovsky's, I don't know.

I decided to paddle up Swan Creek to explore and find out what Swan Lake might be like.

The maps show wild rice beds at the mouth of Swan Creek, but it was mostly a great expanse of pickerelweed at the delta.

I stayed along the shoreline, as I made my way between and over the marshy maze into the creek. A canoe needs only a few inches of water. The sun was bright, so I could perceive where the supportive current flowed between the muddy hummocks that came up nearly to the surface.

Half the width of the creek was choked by submersed vegetation, but the other half, where the flow was, was scoured out.

The water of Swan Creek flows dark. The books call such local waters "tea-colored". I have always referred to them as "coffee-colored". The subjective description must depend on how strong one likes one's tea or how weak one's coffee. (As the dissatisfied cafe customer said to the waitress, "If this is coffee, bring me tea. If this is tea, bring me coffee.")

I didn't feel the current as much resistance to my ascent of Swan Creek. Gusts of wind in certain stretches did surprise me, because I was paddling in the seemingly sheltered low trough of the creek.

Two herons ahead of me would take off at my approach, fly up the creek aways, then alight. As I approached their new standpoint, they would take off again, fly a little farther up the creek, then put down, the same repeated at every curve of the creek. Whenever I have canoed rivers or creeks, I have seen the herons do that. It must not occur to them to fly around behind me, put down and be done with my disturbance once and for all.

The creek was quiet; I had it all to myself. The shallows of marsh at its delta forbid entry of the motorboaters of Pelican Lake.

While in my canoe on the open lake, I am always in peril from unheeding speedboaters who pay me no more mind than they do the waterfowl and would just as soon run me down or swamp me as they fly by. In the creek I felt secure, without such apprehension.

I was in the creek about 45 minutes, when a barrier stopped my upstream progress. A beaver dam stretched across the creek. It was an imposing structure. Judging from the weathered look of its logs, it has been there a long time. Wet mud at its rim indicated recent maintenance.

I peered over it at the dammed pool above, which was several feet higher. A fine project of wetlands creation, accomplished without congressional hearings, environmental impact statements, or taxpayer funding.

I might have dragged my canoe up over the dam to continue on, but I was not in a gung-ho mood. So I never got to see Swan Lake,—the lake I mean. I saw the ballet at the Bolshoi.

No lake, and no swans either. On my return downstream, I did come across a duck, she with two ducklings, a skimpy brood, probably due to those dangers abounding in a predatory world. (Someone told me he witnessed a gull swallow a duckling whole.)

I tried to keep my distance from the mother duck and her two little ones, but the creek was narrow. The mother squawked in alarm and communicated her anxiety to her ducklings.

The three fled downstream before me in hysterical panic, flapping wings, which motion could have carried the mother off into the sky but which availed the ducklings little beyond agitating water under furiously paddling little feet.

The mother duck fell on her side and splashed, feigning injury to draw me away, as the two ducklings fled to cower against the brushy shoreline.

At last, as she judged me far enough downstream from the ducklings, the mother flew back to her little charges, she still squawking in her upset.

I emerged from creek and marsh back onto Pelican Lake, heading to the cabin for lunch.

As in the going-out, so in the coming-back, the usual, the wind in my face.

\* \* \* \* \*

One of the natural attractions of the area is the Orr bog boardwalk.

"What? Bog? Bawg!" you exclaim.

Well, maybe a bog is not that personally attractive to you. Afraid of getting *bogged down*?

The boardwalk will prevent that, don't worry, I assure you.

"Bawg? A frawg on a lawg in a fawg in a bawg," you mock, rejecting the whole idea.

Might you come along if I called the place by its formal name, *Wetlands Interpretive Boardwalk*?

Still no? Well, we naturalists can usually find something attractive in the homeliest settings. As for myself, I've lived the low life in some low places, so a bog might prove congenial to me.

The descriptive words *marsh, bog,* and *swamp* are carelessly used interchangeably, but they are not the same. To my mind, a marsh is a wetland of cattails, dragonflies, tadpoles and frogs, turtles, and red-winged blackbirds, all-inviting to a boy's curious exploratory adventure. A bog, by contrast, is a dark, low morass of acidic stagnant water covered by, smothered by, sphagnum moss, which prevents wholesome oxidation of the water. Only certain rare plants can survive in nutrient-poor, oxygen-deprived, acid water. As for swamp, that belongs in a Florida book, not a Minnesota one.

An informational guide sign at the bog boardwalk states that Minnesota has more bog acreage than all the other forty-seven contiguous states combined. (I don't remember any bogs in Hawaii; Alaska does have muskeg, along with its taiga and tundra.) Most of the Minnesota boglands are here in northern Minnesota, so let that be a caution to your dream of buying land in the great north woods.

The boardwalk itinerary passes through a variety of boggy tree stands: Black ash, tamarack, alder shrub, black spruce—(notice *black* twice). The main interesting feature, however, is in the ground plants that live (if not thrive) in bog conditions.

One of those plants is Labrador tea, from which I might brew a minty tea for myself. Another is water hemlock; if I brewed a tea from that one, the fate of Socrates would be my fate too.

If bog plants are not for general consumption, then how about for some appreciation of beauty-in-miniature? The small purple fringed orchid is an exquisite complex flower the height and breadth of a fingernail.

The first time I took to the Orr bog boardwalk was in late spring, a time that I thought would find the bog all-alive. And so it was,—with mosquitoes. Really, what did I expect? It's stagnant water there, after all. Still, in Brazil I was told that the Amazon lacks mosquitoes because of the acidity of the water; true, I suffered few mosquito bites there. Yet, the Orr bog, acid as it is, was aswarm with mosquitoes, if not bred there, at least resident and ready for blood. Buggy boggy bog! On that occasion, I speedily coursed through the Orr bog boardrun.

My second attempt was in late summer, but the bog at that time, although mostly mosquitoless, appeared still and dull. I traipsed the half-mile loop of the boardwalk finding little of interest, except for the scenic section that ran along the Pelican River.

Today, my third attempt, a July 1st. I chose a day when the gales were roaring, hoping they'd deter the mosquitoes, which are, after all, weak flyers. Lowland as the bog is, although the gales had the tamarack treetops swaying, they did not penetrate at bog-level, except along the river. As it turned out, the mosquitoes must have been in mid-afternoon *siesta*. I needn't have applied the coating of my exposed parts with the chemical repellent.

I set off on the boardwalk.

I wish I had had a bog master to lead me and instruct me, for many of the plants were alien to my dryland naturalist's experience. (And I confess I'm not much of a botanist.) I was surprised to find grass growing out of the sphagnum moss as medium; perhaps the several years of drought have lowered the acid water and enabled grasses, even an occasional dandelion, to take root.

Frustrating my hope, there were few flowers in bloom. The progression of seasonal changes has been accelerated by some warm or hot days during this spring. Nor were the birds there and active.

The boardwalk imposed a raised wooden detachment from the direct experience. I stepped off the boardwalk and trespassed upon the bog itself. The moss was soggy spongy under my feet as expected, but I found solid support where a horizontal tree root underlay the moss. I stepped from hummock to hummock, just far enough on so that I could say that I was in the bog, not just over it. I immersed myself in this experience too, but I kept my feet dry.

What I most wanted to see in the bog was the pitcher plant. Not a plant that throws curve balls and sliders, but one that holds water like a pitcher. And when an insect dips into the pitcher for that water—and something else of alluring taste—, it winds up satisfying the plant's hunger, instead of the bug's thirst. Nutrients below scarce, the pitcher plant sucks them out of the air. Treacherous hospitality!

Search and double-search as I did, I could not find a pitcher plant, even though it was promoted and promised in the brochure.

The pitcher plant is a botanical curiosity much desired by keepers of bizarre houseplants. I suspected poachers of pitchers, but maybe I've just grown too suspicious of human nature, ready to believe the worst.

The host lady back in the Visitor Center insisted that the pitcher plants were there "under the pines". (I saw no pine trees in the bog.) She showed me on the guide map where they were,—the very spot I had gone over twice.

Well, the Nature of any place is not exhausted by a few superficial passings-through. I'll have to go down into the bog again sometime, in my quest for the pitcher plant. Just because I didn't see it doesn't mean it's not there.

\* \* \* \* \*

I knew the general map view of Pelican Lake, but I had not studied it so closely as to memorize the shapes, sizes, and placements of the nearly fifty islands in the lake.

The true shape or size of any island cannot be perceived by just looking at it across the water. From water level, an island presents one face to you. What is on the left flank, on the right, on the back—all perspectives that are out of view?

If you have a map, of course, the contours of an island can be fully perceived and grasped. Even so, a map, fine for orientation, is not good for discovery.

Shouldn't we sometimes venture upon the waters without knowing in advance the details of what is there ahead of us? (We do want to know the way back!)

I set off on another early-morning, calm-water canoe cruise of the north shore of Pelican Lake. I had been up Swan Creek before. I wondered what a farther creek, called Pete's Creek, would be like.

I changed my mind on the destination, when I saw ahead what I recognized as the biggest island in Pelican Lake. Different lake maps give that island different names. You can't rely on lake maps too much. Some maps even admit, "Not intended for navigational use." (No? For what use is a map intended?) Anyway, you have to keep a good part of your navigation in your eyes and between your ears. Look backwards occasionally, because the view coming back is different from the view going out.

A new itinerary now presented itself: Circling around the big island in a loop, then return.

I knew that the island was big, but I had no idea how big, what shape, and what features.

So, paddle on to find out.

A sign on the shore told me that the island is a designated Scientific and Natural Area. No cabins, resorts, or manmade anything on the island (except the signs).

Counterclockwise around the island I went...and went and went. Yes, a very big island.

When I first drew near to the island for comfortable paddling in the shade, I saw two other islands in a line. Well then, when I came around and saw those two islands again, I would know that I had completed my circumnavigation.

As I was going around, I saw islands all over the waterscape.

Three islands appeared in a straight line, but then the last one disappeared behind the other two when I came to a certain position. What I saw as three islands in a cluster turned out on close approach to be only a single island with flanking peninsulas left and right.

Gradual changes in perspective deceive perception. What may appear as a single island might be two, a small one in front of a larger one, but so close that they appear as a single island. Similarly, an island close to the shore might look like a promontory of the mainland. One I saw five minutes before might look like a completely different island now.

When you are canoeing around it, a small island is like a carousel, except that it's not the island that's moving, it's you.

Meanwhile, the big island I was looping showed a receding shoreline,—not the way around, just a big back bay. I shortcut across the opening.

Still more small islands came into the view presented in the limitation of my necessarily narrow straight-on perspective. Several of them lined up. Were they the two that would indicate that I had completed my circumpaddle?

Now, I was not going to keep paddling around and around the big island, my head spinning on the carousel. My compass would prevent that, if I became doubtful on which were the two islands I was looking for. My return had to be northeast; no more westerliness.

When I came around to a northeast bearing, that was the way I would head. And there were indeed two islands of the fifty right there in a line. Even so, I relied on the compass, not the islands, for islands are like people, revealing just one aspect at a time, different aspects at different times, and there is always the possibility of mistaken identity.

To get to know the contours of an island, you have to circumnavigate it. Yes, a map will show you, but interest does not lie in the already known. Interest is in the finding-out for yourself. Too much of our lives is handed to us. We crave the stimulation of discovering the unknowns of islands.

I hurried home in a straight line over empty open water. Threatening clouds coming on behind me.

*****

Back to the bog!

One warm and sunny day, I ventured a return to the Orr bog boardwalk to look for what I hadn't found before. This time I would search with a fine focus.

The small purple fringed orchids were now in full bloom; I closely examined the miniature exquisiteness of their details. Also along the boardwalk were broad patches of jewelweed, the flowers spotted orange cones inviting hummingbirds to dip in to enjoy the nectar.

Halfway on my circuit of the boardwalk I came to the portion along the Pelican River. Examining the cattails and purple loosestrife standing tall on both sides, I failed to see beneath me that the boardwalk there, now afloat upon the river, had been overtopped by the river's water.

Suddenly I found myself on a sideways slide on slime.

Down I thudded onto the hard board.

Having mastered *the slippery rock trick*, I now expanded my clumsy acrobatic repertoire by adding *the slippery boardwalk trick*.

Bruised but unbroken, myself now as soggy as the bog, I struggled back to my feet.

"Immersion in experience", hah!

Oh, the hazards of simple observation of Nature. You've got to look out while looking; focused fascination may make you vulnerable.

Yes, I had read the warning sign at the entrance to the boardwalk: CAUTION. SLIPPERY WHEN WET. The dryness of the early part of the course had made me incautious. I paid the penalty for my heedlessness.

Ribs hurting, I retreated back to the car.

I forgot all about the damn pitcher plant.

At least I hadn't fallen into the river.

\* \* \* \* \*

A slim brown post was topped with a small square plaque upon which was a yellow directional arrow.

It's always good to get a little help to be sure you're starting off in the right direction, I thought to myself, as I took my first hiking steps onto the one-mile loop of the Echo Lake Campground Trail in the Superior National Forest.

I expected to have no trouble following the trail, likely trodden by many of the campers. You don't need to be a native tracker to follow crushed grass or ground worn bare by footfalls.

As I ascended the trail, I came upon a *cairn*, that is, a pile of rocks as a marker, commonly made by separated parties of Native Americans to indicate the way part of the group had taken.

Just up ahead, I saw another cairn, a hip-high stack.

These were not archaeological artifacts, as I could tell by the fresh muddy hollow left where a small boulder had been pulled out of the ground to add to the pile.

As I proceeded, I saw cairn after cairn, each within sight of the next. Were the campground hikers so inept that they needed such frequent indicators of the trail's course?

Then I perceived the rationale for the cairns. The dirt trail frequently passed over wide sloping platforms of bare rock. Arriving there—no evidence of footfalls visible on bare rock—, which way did the trail go? You'd have to circumambulate the rock area to find the resumption of the trail, but, even then, you'd be cast in doubt by an adjacent slab.

I happened to run into a U.S. Forest Service overseer of the campground and trail. He it was, he told me, who had directed some summer interns to the heaping-up of guiding rock piles.

I acknowledged their usefulness to him, yet I had found myself looking ahead, not to whatever natural feature or creature I might encounter, but to the next cairn. My main visual impression was of a succession of rock piles one after another. It was as if the trail became subsidiary to the trail markers.

Persisting in my usual mode of trying to find my way on my own, I came across a pile of dead saplings and branches sprawled over what I thought was the trail. But, no, a cairn stood out on an eminence in another direction. The Forest Service interns must have laid the saplings-and-branches obstacle to prevent a going-off-course mistake that I myself was about to make.

The Forest Service wants hikers to stick to the trail, not only so they don't get lost (a human concern), but so that they won't trample all over, and degrade, the vegetation (an environmental concern). The cairns keep hikers on the trail; what keeps them from trampling the vegetation is a posted warning that includes two words powerful against waywardness: "Poison Ivy".

The highlight of the trail was the high point,—a rock platform at the level of the treetops on the far horizon. There is an exhilaration in mere physical presence in a high place with a broad sweep of overlook.

When, after cairn to cairn, I finished the hike, arriving at the end of the loop, I wondered about the difference between giving helpful guidance on the one hand, and leading around by the nose. I suppose parents must similarly wonder about that difference as they take on the upbringing of their children....

I drove less than a mile east on the Echo Trail to what is called the Hunter's Walking Trail.

Just before the beginning of that trail was a characteristic phenomenon of the local limnology. The tannin stained water from a large bog to my right was spilling into a culvert, on its way to some local river or lake.

I don't know why nature writers try to make bog water sound potable and palatable by comparing it to coffee or tea. My beverage of choice to describe this bog outflow was root beer, accurate even to the foam at the spill into the culvert. Root beer, but still, I wouldn't drink it.

The Hunter's Walking Trail might on this summer day be better described as the Raspberry Picker's Harvest Trail. The fruit-laden canes were cordons to the trail.

It soon became apparent to me that what I was on was not hiking trail but Forest Service road, which had been well-trodden by tread. Not recently though, as I could tell by so much clover, wildflowers, and grasses on the trail itself that I thought I was walking through a cow pasture, complete with butterflies and bumblebees.

The trail proceeded level and straight or gently curving to accommodate vehicles. It was edged by shrubs and dark, dense undergrowth, in all, the continued lowlandedness of the bog. The deerflies harried me all the way.

Offshoot loops branched from the trail, the whole adding up to more than nine miles. The sameness of it all sent me retracing my steps after thirty minutes.

As happens on hikes, I saw on the way back what I had not seen on the way out.

First, organic crudity evidence—right in the middle of the path, how had I missed it?—that the moose is not wholly extinct in Minnesota. Some have compared such evidence to Tater Tots, a simile that must be most displeasing to the makers of processed potatoes for human consumption. As one would expect from such a large animal, these moose Tater Tots were a platterful. They looked old and dry, past their shelf life.

In the same category, I next came across wolf scat, distinguishable from that of dog by the deer or moose hair in the composition. This deposit was also dried out and old.

If I surmised a scenario or episodic link between the producers of the two scat piles, it would be, based on the condition of the evidence, a stale wildlife story.

The forest around the Hunter's Walking Trail is a designated grouse management area, patches cut out to provide congenial habitat for the bird. Eyes open and ears alert, I neither saw nor heard any grouse. Anyway, earlier in the day, I had inadvertently flushed a covey of eight or ten grouse while walking down Slade Road near my own cabin. Grouse in my area evidently manage without management.

The looking-for-without-finding and the finding-without-looking-for remind me of a complaint I have heard from a hunter friend of mine: "When I go turkey hunting, I see no turkeys but lots of deer. When I go deer hunting, I see no deer but lots of turkeys."

"Why don't you take up golf?" I advised him. "The holes are always there."

*  *  *  *  *

Before setting out on a hike, the first thing to consider is the weather, not only the prospects for inclemency, but also whether conditions conduce to pleasant walking. A hot and muggy day, for example, can turn an enjoyable stroll into a sweaty, slogging forced march, especially when there is much uphill/downhill in the course.

Today was the ideal hiking day, temperatures from the mid-60°s to the mid-70°s, with a constant stiff breeze to refresh and to blow away the bugs.

We have had some heavy rains recently, but this rock-floor landscape drains away its rainfall quickly.

– – –(Regarding drainage: Sixty miles south of my cabin is a three-way continental divide. A raindrop on one slope there may proceed to Lake Superior and eventually to the Atlantic, on another slope to the Mississippi River and on to the Gulf of Mexico, on another slope through northern lakes and rivers to Hudson Bay.)– – –

As I knew from previous hikes there, the Vermilion Gorge Trail is a mostly upland itinerary, without standing water to plod through. (Draining raindrops there head for Hudson Bay.)

The U.S. Forest Service has laid out many attractive hiking trails. There is a lot to be said for hiking on a laid-out trail. Difficult passages may be made easier,—a boardwalk over standing water, logs or planks crossing holes, a flight of steps on steep inclines. Also, you can be confident that the course was chosen to display interesting natural features and scenic perspectives.

If following a laid-out course seems too tame or conformist to you, well, then, you're welcome to go bushwhacking. *Bushwhacking* in this sense doesn't mean hiding behind a boulder and shooting someone off a horse. Northwoods bushwhacking is whacking your way through the bush. (Hereabouts we don't say, "I'm going into the woods." We say, "I'm going into the bush.")

You've seen the movies of explorers and natives bushwhacking through tropical jungle, hacking and whacking with a machete. (I used to live in tropical Brazil and owned a machete. The only whacking I did with it was into a coconut for a refreshing drink on my veranda.)

I don't think a machete would work well in a Minnesota alder thicket or on close-by-side fir trees. Some of the forest and bog here is impenetrable, except to the most fanatic bushwhackers.

My fishing partners and I were once camped on a Quetico lake. Studying the map, we saw, not far from our location, a small lake, unnamed, without portage trail to it. The most fervent fantasy of a fisherman is to fish virgin waters. Was that little lake virginal, fishwise?

Hey, it didn't look very far. We could bushwhack to it! All we had to do was follow the compass bearing.

The compass bearing led us to a sheer unscalable rock face. Around that, on track again, into an ankle-deep bog. Then into bug-infested scrub. We wasted a good part of the day, never got to the little lake, and turned back to where we had already been catching a lot of fish. Bushwhacking!

The trailhead of the Vermilion Gorge Trail is at the end of the road in the town that is the literal end of the road, Crane Lake, Minnesota. Canada is just beyond Crane Lake, and that part of Canada is roadless woods and waters. To venture on from Crane Lake you have to abandon the car and board a boat or a floatplane. I myself was only on a three-mile round-trip saunter still within the United States.

A pair of flickers were feeding their fledged offspring in the middle of the trail. Flickers are a kind of woodpecker, but why should they rattle their brains knocking on wood for grubs, when the ground is aswarm with ants that can be plucked up without headache? There never seems to be a shortage of ants.

Many predator insects and birds do not dine on ants, because ants secrete formic acid, rendering them too spicy for most tastes. Not so the flickers. They are like people who pour the hot chili pepper sauce liberally on their meal. (One naturalist I read recommends the formic acid seasoning of ants. Pick up an ant, bite off its head, and enjoy the body!, he urged. Not for me. I grew up on bland food.)

As I was watching the flickers, I heard somewhere high above me in the trees a robin.

We think of robins as town dwellers, plucking earthworms out of our mowed lawns and nesting near, or on, our buildings. So it was that I was surprised the first time I detected a robin here in the north woods; it seemed misplaced in the wild.

Robins here present a character different from the familiar. I may hear a robin, but, if I see one, it acts wary and elusive. In towns, robins tolerate human presence; here they avoid and flee humans. In the wild, robins are wild. What is their authentic nature,— urbanized/suburbanized or wild? Whichever, their adaptability is why robins are so widespread and abundant.

Ahead of me a red fox vixen pranced daintily down the path, then, turning aside, she gave me a bushytailed bye.

Along the Vermilion Gorge Trail were signs informative of the economic history of the area. In the mid-17th century began the fur trade, to the near extinction of the beaver, fisher, marten, muskrat, mink, and otter. Next, in the mid-19th, was mining, gold briefly, then iron continuing to today. Last was logging, most of the old-growth pines of northern Minnesota cut down in only 35 years. The old-growth stands of the Boundary Waters were reduced from 25% to 4% of the land area. Fur trade, mining, and logging,—all exploitive, devouring spoliation.

Tacked to a tree along the trail was a yellow cardboard folded like a pup tent, both ends open. "Gypsy Moth Survey." Gypsy moths, an environmental scourge, along with the spruce budworm, the woolly adelgid, the emerald ash borer, and others of the sinister havocs. Peeking into the trap, I saw one dead spider and a dead ant, two innocents, and contributing nothing to research besides.

I ascended to the high ridge over the Vermilion River.

I found there an accommodating bench. I sat down and rested beneath the tall pines in a small grove. I attempted some Buddhist meditation, but only found myself hypnotized by the pendulum swaying of the tops of the pines in the strong winds.

I then descended to a boat dock on the river. The Vermilion River there completes its forty-mile flow from Vermilion Lake to Crane Lake.

A white scum on the surface was blown against the shore and filled a cove. Little blocks of detergent suds looked like miniature icebergs in the flow. Phosphates, I suspect.

I took the return at my usual leisurely pace, spending some more time on the bench, trying for attunement. Relatedness to Nature should not be a series of mere impressions or episodes, but, rather, a constant state of being, an attunement.

I had the trail all to myself, except for the very end, when I passed in approach a couple with two teenage boys. The man was a logo billboard mannequin. His hat, his vest, his shirt announced his patronage of the most upscale haberdashers for the outdoors. He also carried a store-bought decorated walking stick, a necessary implemental accompaniment to his outfit. A fine specimen of regalia, he was.

Meanwhile, the teenage boys, identical twins I

think they were, dawdled behind. I got the impression that they would have liked to be receiving a more stimulating entertainment. Their apathetic relation to Nature is a common contemporary attitude, so different from the eager adventurousness I felt at their age....

I then drove seven miles to Vermilion Falls, where a foaming and frothing A & W flow gushes its way through the narrow constriction of black granite walls. It is an impressive sight of rushing river impelled by gravity.

Unlike the national parks of the West, these Minnesota Superior National Forest trails are not overrun by hordes of people. I encountered only a mother-and-daughter blueberry picking team, a husband and wife, the latter in a wheelchair, and a sociable couple from Cass Lake.

I sat at a picnic table and had my lunch.

Then, from the rock point below the falls, I caught two fat smallmouth bass. (I am not so doddering as to need a walking stick, but I sometimes do hike with a fishing rod.)

A garter snake slithered across a bare boulder on the bank. Exposed, she was vulnerable to attack from an aerial predator, but, after a minute or so on the sun-warmed rock, she made it safely down into the concealment of the grass.

Unusual for a snake, garters are northland hardy. Even so, they face the challenge of finding a freeze-free hibernation refuge.

There are no poisonous snakes to cause anxiety to local hikers.

I later ventured down the portage trail that bypasses the Vermilion River where it shoots the chutes. I had no canoe to carry over this portage; just my exploratory curiosity.

* * * * *

It would be as unfeasible to canoe Pelican Lake's fifty-mile periphery of shoreline as it would be to hike it. If you're beguiled by weed-choked bays and coves, I suppose you could do it, and if you had days and nights and were willing to pitch your tent amidst bug-infested brush, on a rock top, steep slope, or on the lawn of someone's summer cabin.

I know so little of this huge lake, so I thought I should take on a daylong excursion. I chose a course of about seven miles.

Vigorous paddling speed is like average brisk walking speed, about three miles an hour, if wind is not a factor of consideration. (Wind is always a factor.)

The weather report gave me blue skies and a wind out of the west at 10-to-15 miles an hour. I would have preferred 5-to-10 and would not have ventured out if I heard 20-to-30. (If I waited for calm, my canoe would never get wet.)

My chosen course being east, then south, I thought a west wind, if wind there must be, the most favorable. I was going to follow the shoreline from the cabin, then east into Orr Bay, a narrow straight north-south bay, then south into the Pelican River down to its dam.

You might compute that, if my course was about seven miles and average canoeing speed is three miles an hour, what kind of all-day trip was that?

My objective was not to fill a day with hard paddling, but to get to know the lake better. A very leisurely pace is necessary for that purpose.

With lunch and rain gear—(blue sky now, who knows what later?)—I set out from the little cove near my cabin.

The wind in actuality was out of the southwest.

If there are whitecaps on a big lake, a canoeist should not venture out onto open water. I did not see whitecaps at first, but later there were to be white feathers.

It's a good canoe trip when the most strenuous or trying part of it is at the beginning, when the canoeist is strong and alert. When fatigue sets in, neither body nor mind meets difficulties well.

The waves came down the whole length of the lake toward me. They were swells, some of which broke.

My canoe has no keel, which makes it fast, but, on the other hand, tippy. However, when I canoe alone, I have a center seat to sit on, balancing the canoe bow to stern and preventing the wind from spinning me. I wield a kayak paddle, which enables keeping a true course without tossing the paddle from left to right and back again.

Out on the open water now, the waves bearing down upon me, I felt unsteady as the canoe bobbed. I didn't consider myself endangered, but there was just enough uncertainty to cause a bit of that stomach weightlessness one experiences on roller coasters.

During the push of the paddle stroke, the canoe feels secure. The dig into the water is like a hand grabbing and holding. When the paddle is out of the water between strokes, however, the bobbing can be unsettling.

I tried to keep the bow quartered to the wind, but it was difficult. My apprehension slowed me down, I paying more attention to the pattern of the incoming waves than to Oak Point, around which I would pass.

After a half-hour of paddling, during which I had turned about toward shore, attempting to let the waves carry me—even if that lengthened my course—, I felt more uneasy. If not whitecaps, there were those white feathers.

I dropped off the seat onto my knees to lower my center of gravity. I immediately felt a better, more secure control.

The waves crashed against Oak Point as I passed it and headed east.

It would seem that I should have had an easier time now, the wind behind me. I didn't need to paddle much, true, but the wind that propelled me was also pushing against the side of the stern, trying to swing me about broadside. The disadvantage of the seat in the middle is much diminished rudder control compared to sitting in the stern. I had to hold the long kayak paddle at its off end and put muscle into the corrections.

The lake map lay on the canoe bottom in front of me. Still a beginner with GPS, I've done little more than mark the Point as my waypoint #1. In lieu of satellitical electronic direction, I was following the old-fashioned canoeist's method of point-to-point navigation and use of the compass.

– – –(I heard about a fisherman who accidentally dropped his GPS overboard. The fisherman's mouth also dropped. He looked around and discovered that he had no idea where on the expansive chain of lakes he was. He wound up spending the night sleeping on the deck of his boat, rescue arriving only the next afternoon, when a well-piloted boat happened by.)– – –

It takes a while to correlate the map scale to what you see in front of you. Which point of the several I saw ahead was the one for the turn?

The course of this excursion was elementary-level; I couldn't get lost.

At last, the opening to Orr Bay, between Ambassador Point and Indian Point, was obvious before me.

As soon as I turned south at Indian Point, a wooded peninsula blocked the wind, and I was becalmed. Lunch time, afloat.

Boats filled with family groups from the resorts floated here and there throughout Orr Bay. Motorboaters consider canoeists oddities; some stared at me, as if wondering how I could possibly get anywhere over the water under my own power.

One man even shouted at me, "Hey, you forgot your motor!"

To which I responded, "My heart is my motor."

I slowly paddled down the lee western shore of Orr Bay, the town of Orr opposite me on the east. The view of Orr from the water in the bay is nothing impressive like the view of the skyscrapers of Chicago from Lake Michigan, but the perspective idea is the same.

Out on a dock at the south end of Orr Bay stood a boy, ten or eleven years old, fishing.

"Catch anything today?" I asked him.

No, he answered, but he said he expected to.

I saw that he was flinging a ridiculously oversize lure. I suggested he use something smaller.

No, he declined my suggestion. He told me that he had seen a "really, really big" northern pike hanging around the dock. That was the fish he was going to catch, and he needed a very big lure to catch him, he said.

I knew that the "really, really big" northern pike have been long gone from Pelican Lake. I was urging the boy to fish with practicality and efficiency. He rejected my advice, because he was fishing with his imagination.

At last, I was in the beginning of the Pelican River. It lay wide and shallow, little apparent current at first. There was extensive submersed and emergent aquatic vegetation, especially patches of lilies, both the yellow and the white, some few flowered, many about to.

A swath of clear water extended down the center of the river.

I had left behind the commotion of dockside Orr and the boats motoring around the bay. There was no one to be seen on the shore and no other craft of any kind in the river. I was not paddling much now, just drifting, idling in a near trance.

I passed the riverfront section of the Orr bog boardwalk, where I had explored (and suffered mishap) a short while before. The river from the boardwalk then, the boardwalk from the river now. Reverse of perspective is a good technique for a naturalist. (I used to have my apprentice naturalists stand with their backs to a lake, bend over and view through their legs blue lake as blue sky and vice versa; and were the clouds now islands?)

The submersed weeds gradually took on a down-river bend. Even so, it was wind rather than current that most moved me.

I didn't remember that the Pelican River passes under Nett Lake Road before it gets to the dam. I had neglected to check out the situation of that passage. I now found a three-part pass-through under the road, with drops off a concrete ledge.

No rock bouncing for me. I pulled the canoe up onto the bank, got out, walked the half-mile to where I had left my car, brought the car to the canoe, lifted the canoe atop it, secured all, and drove back to the cabin.

\* \* \* \* \*

The next day, a continuation of the previous itinerary:

I put on my life jacket and slid the canoe through the high grass down into the Pelican River below the dam on Highway 53. Holding on to each gunwale, I stepped into the canoe, took my middle seat, picked up my paddle, and was afloat.

Just in front of me, a railroad crew was doing track repairs on the bridge. It is important to keep that line operational, for it is the means by which Canada gets rid of its natural resources.

Ducking my head, I passed under the railroad bridge.

Once the traffic sounds of Highway 53 are left behind, you can drift down the Pelican River imagining it the Nile, taking the water lilies for lotus and the sedges on the margins for papyrus.

My plan was to spend the morning ascending the small river that enters the Pelican from the south, then the afternoon descending the Pelican River itself.

The sky was cloudless blue, the temperature forecast in the low 80°s, a cool breeze blowing out of the west, in all, prospects for a pleasant day of canoeing.

It wasn't long before I got to the river entering from the south. The water was dark with tannin leached from the decaying vegetation of the bogs. (Let's have no more talk of coffee, tea, or root beer!)

The grass stems underwater leaned with the slight current, indicating the direction of flow, at the same time that their emergent blades bent like crooked forefingers pointing wherever the wind directed them.

There were water lilies, too, both the yellow and the white. The pads were of remarkable size; I measured one 16-1/2" in diameter. Not the huge *Victoria regia* of the Amazon, which you could almost walk upon—(some local birds there do that)—, but a tropical touch for the northland milieu, nonetheless.

The river was bordered on both sides by a lowland from which emerged tall grasses and sedges with their roots in water. The woods rose well back behind those wide margins.

Were you in the canoe with me, you might have exclaimed, "What's all your talk about this being 'the land of rock'? There's not a boulder, stone, or pebble visible anywhere. Everything is soft and green."

"You're right. General descriptions do not apply to every little locale in the area," I would concede.

The red-winged blackbird cocks were conducting their aerial skirmishes over the grass margins. Territory and females, two common instigators of conflict between males. And the male red-winged blackbird is a land-grabbing, promiscuous chap.

Once again, I had the river all to myself, but there was one instance of cross-traffic. A muskrat was swimming across the river in front of me. When he perceived that I would not yield, he dove under and sped ahead to avoid collision.

I had forgotten my watch, but what did clock time matter? These early summer days are long; they will not soon shut down daytime excursions.

So, was it an hour or 45 minutes later that I arrived into Rice Lake?

None of the 21 Minnesota bodies of water named *Rice Lake* is named after Mr. Rice. No, it is wild rice that provides the descriptive designation.

If your idea of a lake is an expanse of open water, Rice Lake will disappoint. It is, instead, an expanse of aquatic vegetation overlying the water beneath. Floridian almost.

The main plant was pickerelweed, which I had always mistakenly called arrowhead. The name *arrowhead* was already taken by another aquatic plant, one I would better describe as *lancehead*. My plant has the stereotypical arrowhead form, the pointed tip and spread knuckles on the bottom. Well, at least my plant didn't get stuck with the name of a similar, *duck potato.*

- - -(Common names of plants and animals can be confusing. Why should there be *pickerelweed* in an area where the chain pickerel, the species of fish referred to, is totally absent? No pickerels to be found lurking among those weeds. (And, when a Canadian says *pickerel*, he means walleye.) The locals may call grouse *partridges*, herons *cranes* or even *pelicans*. Too bad that when Adam bestowed names upon all the creatures of the earth there was no available secretary to record the names. One of the books of the Old Testament should have been a field guide.)- - -

Many of the white water lilies in the lake were in full flower, the yellow core contrasting with the bright white petals. Beauty but only the faintest perfume.

I presume that some of the grasses in and around Rice Lake must be wild rice. (Wild rice is not a rice, but a grass.) As the grasses have not yet fully matured and seeded, I did not recognize the wild rice.

You'd never think of a canoe as an agricultural vehicle, but it is the one of choice for the harvest of wild rice. A canoe will float on the shallowest of water, so it can go to and among the wild rice.

The procedure is this: One person in the canoe bends the wild rice stalks over the canoe with a paddle. The other person flails the stalks with a stick, knocking the grains to the bottom of the canoe. That was the Native American way; I don't know of a more practicable one that will collect the wild rice without killing the plant.

I returned down to the confluence with the Pelican River, dropped a small mushroom anchor in the middle, and had my floating lunch.

The railroad repair crew too must have been at their lunch, for the diesel roar and the hammering of their machines had ceased. A midday stillness fell over the river.

But now the wind picked up. It blew by me at a steady flow, then increased in briskness.

I heard a sweet sustained high-pitched tone, barely discernable but seemingly quite near me. What was it? Perhaps tinnitus, a ringing-in-the-ears, a sound only within my own head?

No, it was something else.

I looked in the river, along the banks, and into the air. Nothing there that could have made the sound. I turned my head this way and that, listening hard, trying to narrow down to the source.

My fishing rod stood straight up in the canoe, leaning against the gunwale. The sound was coming from my fishing rod.

The fishing line ran through all the eyes of the rod to the tip, then back down again to an eye near the handle, where my lure was hooked. I had reeled the line taut, so that the lure would not come loose and dangle about in the canoe.

The wind was blowing across that taut line and sounding that faint sweet tone.

I had discovered an instance of the *Aeolian harp*, a natural music made by a wire or line set vibrating by wind.

Aeolus, god of the winds, a musician!

I drew close to my fishing rod and listened intently to the tone.

Then I began to wonder: This rod was seven-feet long and produced that particular pitch. I had other rods of different lengths,—six-foot, five-, and four-foot-nine-inches. If, with each rod strung up line taut, I put them side-by-side upright in my canoe on a day when

Aeolus wanted to perform, would each strung rod produce a different pitch according to the length of the exposed fishing line? And wouldn't all the pitches combine into a harmony?

A symphony orchestra is composed of brasses, percussion, strings, and winds. My fishing line Aeolian orchestra would be composed of two of those four,— strings produced by winds.

The *music of the spheres* may be too far away to be heard, but the Aeolian harp is near and available for our musical pleasure....

Dense cumulus clouds were now rolling in from the west, promising some afternoon shade. (That promise is not always kept. Some days, substantial clouds travel every portion of the sky, yet the sunshine is uninterrupted.)

Downstream now, but still a weak current.

No lily pads or pickerelweeds in this river; open water from margin to margin.

A car-size white boulder lay along one side, answering my imaginary partner's earlier objection to my characterization of the topography.

I passed under an old rusted iron bridge, its roadway creosote-soaked ties covered with gravel. When I stood up in the canoe and grabbed hold of the bridge to examine it, the creosote smell filled my nostrils and made me recoil.

A few hills overlook the Pelican River; houses and pole barns perch upon them. I passed a couple working on the outside of their new (or rebuilt) riverside cabin. The man was on the roof attaching tin sheeting, the woman bringing more sheets below. (His work didn't seem successful, for, when I retraced my course later, I saw him tearing up what he had laid down.)

The couple's big dog had already acquired a proprietary attitude. As I paddled past, he ran down to the bank, snarling and barking viciously at me. Had he entered the river and come after me, I would have expressed my own proprietary attitude by cracking the paddle upon his noggin.

In the river margins of standing grasses fluttered a greater variety of damselflies and dragonflies than the bluet damselflies I've come across almost everywhere on water or land. One damselfly, the river jewelwing, especially abundant, showed black-tipped wings and a striking slim shining metallic emerald body. The damselflies are river sprites.

A hawk hurried over the river, being harassed and mobbed by blue jays. The jays sounded the general alarm and shrieked out the attack call. Other jays from the nearby woods heard and responded by joining the mob. Sometimes the predators are subjected to the turnabout of suffering pursuit.

The paddling was pleasant, all downstream and through open water. At times, the woods now came right up to the water's edge.

I felt the flow beneath me becoming stronger, the river width contracted. Rock riffles lay ahead.

This Pelican River will join the Vermilion River, then into Crane Lake, Sand Point, Namakan, and Rainy lakes and onward north into Hudson Bay.

No such protracted itinerary was on my mind. I decided to turn back. I would have to paddle against both current and a now-much-stiffer wind. I dealt with both by making my return paddling along the grassy margin.

\* \* \* \* \*

To get to know a river, you can canoe its entirety, from point-of-origin to ultimate immersion into another river, a lake, or a sea. A river is flow. If you yourself flow with that flow, you will become, in a sense, one with the river, the flow of your life merging into the flow of the river.

A lake called Itasca, here in Minnesota, spills out into a clear shallow creek. I once took off my shoes and socks and stepped into the cold outflow of Lake Itasca. There, right there, is the point-of-origin of the Mississippi River.

I stepped into that flow, but I could not put in my canoe and continue down the entire length of the Mississippi River unto its ultimate end. How could I portage all the locks and dams? How could I survive in a canoe among the barging barges and all the other fearsome traffic on the Mississippi? And so, what I know of the Mississippi is a here-and-there acquaintance acquired in my various travels.

Locally, I have found the point-of-origin of our Pelican River and flowed with its early course. Then, beyond the dam, I canoed several miles of its continuation. The riffles and rapids ensuing discouraged me from participating in the full flow of the Pelican River from start to finish.

What about that finish? The Pelican River flows into the Vermilion. Couldn't I access the end of the Pelican River from its confluence with the Vermilion?

On the road to Crane Lake lies a hamlet called Buyck. The locals there, obviously tired of answering one particular question, have affixed a child's bicycle to the sign that announces the town's name.

There is a bridge over the Vermilion River in Buyck and, next to the bridge, a put-in for canoes. On the morning of a warm sunny Sunday, I launched my canoe there for the five-mile downstream paddle to the confluence of the Vermilion and the Pelican.

The Vermilion River is tannin-tinted, but the water quality is most wholesome. We have so abused the rivers of North America that it is heartening to find a healthy one.

I had scouted the river the day before, concerned that heavy recent rains may have swollen and accelerated the flow to the consequence of grueling labor on my upstream paddle-back. Yes, the Vermilion was in full flow, but not so much as to overmaster my strength.

When I returned on the Sunday morning, I found that most of the runoff had run through and the river was more relaxed.

The Vermilion there is a scenic river, broad and smooth, lined with tall grasses that extend back into marshes or, elsewise, forest trees to the margin.

On the way down, the current carried me along; I needed to make only slight corrections in the steering.

As I went on and on, past curves left and right, ever more water ahead, I wondered whether I might have taken on too strenuous a canoeing course. Late middle age doubts itself.

At last, after 2-1/2 hours of some paddling, some steering, but mostly just drifting with the flow (all the while apprehensive about the paddling labor I would have to expend on my return), I arrived at the confluence of the Vermilion with the Pelican.

I turned into the Pelican River and ascended.

The flow was coated with white scum and suds, the Pelican apparently a source of what I had seen at the Vermilion's arrival at Crane Lake.

It was only a short way to the rapids.

I pulled the canoe out at the base of the rapids, at the designated portage path. I climbed the bare rock hill to look upon the churning, boiling descent of the Pelican River.

Staring down into these rapids, I recalled a day long ago. I was in my canoe in the Boundary Waters, anchored in the flow of the Basswood River. A bright orange bulk came floating by. A life jacket, unworn. I hoped that it only had been dropped overboard upstream. I fished it out. Back at the outfitters, I was told that some adventurers thought they could run something called Wheelbarrow Falls. One man drowned. The life jacket was his property.

As in life, so in a flowing river it is not the rocks you see but those you don't see that might do you in. A canoeist had better learn to read water. Any anomaly in the surface indicates something solid just below. An upwelling and a curtain cascade toward you mean a submerged rock face that would stop a canoe with a crash, flip it about, and likely batter and drown any foolhardy reckless who thought they could "run the rapids".

A big snapping turtle was sunning herself on the bare rock. Seeing me, she withdrew her head at my intrusion. I left her alone and turned away, heading to a shady spot for my lunch.

I immediately came upon a turtle nest in a small patch of the rare diggable dirt. The shallow nest had been sniffed out, dug up, and the eggs eaten by some marauding creature of the night. The emptied shells, all shriveled up, lay scattered about in the dirt. No hatchlings emerged from that clutch to carry on the species into another generation.

I looked back upon the sunning turtle. If she was the one who laid those eggs, her procreative effort had failed.

Back in my canoe, I returned to the confluence with the Vermilion, the *end* of the Pelican River, although, of course, its waters, now mingling with those of the Vermilion, would continue on through the watershed.

You might enter a point-of-origin of a river, like my step into the outflow of Lake Itasca. However, you cannot find the terminus of a river, because the flow never ends. A freshet into a rivulet, a rivulet into a brook, a brook into a creek, a creek into a stream, a stream into a river, a river into a larger river, that larger river into a lake, then a further spillover into another river, on and on, eventually into the sea. Nor is the sea the terminus of a river, for evaporation lifts out of the sea what had been river water and carries it back inland, where it rains down, the runoff eventually into a river and so back into the cycle.

Not only don't I know the Pelican River start to finish, I don't know, can't know, any river that way. There may be a start, but there is no finish.

We may canoe a river, flow in the flow, over some few stretches, but immersion in the full flow of the cycle-of-waters must always be beyond us.

I know from experience the start of the Pelican River and its end as shown on a map. Beyond the confluence I must necessarily remain in experiential ignorance.

My upstream paddle-back of the Vermilion took almost the exact same amount of time as my descent. Apparently, I was not slowed down by the current, by my age, or by my riverine contemplations.

* * * * *

I climbed a hill where, the day before, I had discovered extensive patches of wild raspberries, the fruit fully ripe and in profusion.

I carried with me a bowl to hold my takings. Like the birds (and bears), I would harvest what I never planted. Nature's open-air market is available to all the creatures of the earth. We naturalists, undeserving beneficiaries as we are, don't disdain a handout.

Unshaded by any tall trees, the raspberry canes could rise above—or stand beside—the wildflowers, weeds, and shrubs around them, all in amicable sharing of the full sun on the hilltop.

There was a stony path, with wide ruts, where all-terrain vehicles have passed. I found fewer raspberries along that path than off back from it. Perhaps a bear on the path had made the same discovery of raspberry bounty as I had. As I picked, I looked back over my shoulder from time to time.

Of course, I tasted a few raspberries as I gathered them for the bowl. I tried (but failed) to follow the rule I used to lay down to the children in my Nature class when I conducted a wild fruit harvest: "Eat one, pick nine."

Like all wild fruits, these raspberries were smaller than our cultivated varieties, very seedy too. The full flavor is derived by chewing the seeds while squeezing the juice from the pulp between tongue and palate.

When I had accumulated an inch layer in the bowl, I drew the bowl under my nose and inhaled the distinctive raspberry fragrance.

My intention was to take my bowl of raspberries back to the cabin to mix the fruit into vanilla ice cream.

Wild raspberries, nourishment provided wholly by Nature. No hand of man involved, except my own in the free-for-the-taking.

Then, ice cream, made from the milk of domesticated cattle, sugar raised on a plantation, the final processed product enabled by the technology of refrigeration. The hand of man not only involved, but creating that which does not, could not, exist in Nature.

Back at the cabin, I mixed wild raspberries into the vanilla ice cream and enjoyed the happy combination.

How representative that was of so many aspects of the content of human life,—what Nature provides enriched by what the ingenuity of man has created. Our human life is so much more bountiful than are the lives of the other creatures on earth, they who must live wholly within Nature's provisioning.

\* \* \* \* \*

A few days of saturating rains have provoked the eruption and erection of the mushrooms.

Actually, the mushrooms are always there, underground. What comes up is the generative organ that produces spores, the seeds of new mushroom colonies. The visible mushrooms are suddenly there, discharge their function, and then shrink and wither away.

Mushrooms are not a vegetable; they are a fungus. They are ugly, slimy, have little taste and negligible nutrition. We love them.

At our sometime peril. A mushroom just emerged outside my cabin window is the curiously named fly agaric, or, in Latin nomenclature, *Amanita muscaria*. It is a yellow-golden white-stippled globular dome upon a white stalk. The dome plumps out into an umbrella, to the excitement of the sex-crazed Freudians.

**"HIGHLY POISONOUS"** warns my field guide in bold print.

I wonder what the physiological consequences are from consuming "slightly poisonous", or "moderately poisonous", or **"HIGHLY POISONOUS"**. (I wonder, but my curiosity is not nagging me to conduct an experiment.)

A naturalist learns by using all the senses, but, in the case of the fly agaric, one sense had better be left out. Other mushrooms in the *Amanita* family are named *destroying angel* and *death cap*. What a family.

The symptoms menu after consuming some *Amanita* mushrooms includes dry mouth or excessive salivation, slowed or difficult breathing, nausea, vomiting, diarrhea, confusion, excitability, stupor, and hallucinations. Oh, and possible coma and death.

Warnings and cautions aside, I pick mushrooms, anyway... from a supermarket produce display or a tin can. Sight, smell, and touch are all the senses I put to work on mushrooms in the field.

Whatever the role of the mushroom in the human erotic mind, the role of the mushroom and other fungi in Nature is decomposition of organic material.

If you are so foolhardy as to munch upon some *Amanita* mushrooms, you may suffer decomposition of your own organic material.

\* \* \* \* \*

In this "Land of 10,000 Lakes", you can no more assume that one lake is just like another than, picking a random sample of 10,000 people, you would expect to find them identical. Age, gender, race, looks, build, personality, mannerisms, voice, language, and life experience distinguish one human from another. People have the commonality of humanness, of course. Lakes have the commonality of water; beyond that, just as with people, lakes are distinguishable by many differentiators.

Each lake has its area, shape, depths, bottom contour and composition, liquid volume, and shoreline physiognomy. So, the solid geometry of a body of water.

A more significant difference among lakes is basic chemistry: Acidity/alkalinity as expressed in pH, suspended or dissolved elements and minerals (some brought in by inlets), and, unfortunately, contaminants and pollutants (not only toxic mercury but lawn fertilizer from shorelines).

Sunlight penetration is different in each lake, due to the clarity of the water and the variations of depths. The chemical nature of the water reacts to that sunlight penetration, as well as to temperature conditions determined by weather and climate, to create the particular community of aquatic life. Lakes may be fertile, infertile, or, in worst case, acidic and sterile.

My own Pelican Lake is mostly shallow, which results in sunlight penetration that produces extensive submersed and emergent vegetation. Except for bare boulders underwater along the shoreline, what you see when you look down into Pelican Lake is not the bottom, but masses and varieties of aquatic vegetation. As a consequence, Pelican is full of life, from the basic phytoplankton and zooplankton through the insects, mollusks, crustaceans, fish, amphibians, reptiles, birds, and mammals,—a cornucopia of aquatic and aquatic-dependent life-forms. Pelican Lake is extremely fertile, aphrodisiacal to naturalists and fishermen.

I put my canoe atop my car for a half-hour drive to a lake named Kjostad. (In pronouncing the name, you should not sound like you are choking; the beginning of the name is like the second syllable of a sneeze.)

Kjostad Lake is 400 acres, a suitable size for daylong exploration by canoe. The lake is long on the east-west axis and has two islands.

The big island is covered solid and dense with trees, including magnificent pines. That island presents the vast north woods on the scale of an acre. The nearby small island is just a rock hump with a half-dozen forlorn weather-beaten trees.

What struck me first when I entered upon Kjostad was how much of the bottom I could see in the shallows and how much of a sandy barren that bottom was. The water is tinted brown, but there was little apparent algae or suspended vegetation such as fills the green murky waters of Pelican Lake.

Kjostad has some deep holes, up to 50 feet. At such a depth, sunlight fails to reach any would-be rooted vegetation. Most of the main basin of Kjostad is open water.

I paddled into the shallows of the big bays and did find there heavy mats of water shield, a kind of lily with small elliptical pads, the bottoms of which were slimy to the touch. In some coves, the pads fit closely together, like a mosaic, providing a roof of shade to the frogs and fish sheltered below. The water shield was confined to the bays and coves of the lake.

How silent Kjostad Lake was! A bright sunny summer day, and yet I was the only human upon the waters. It's not that Kjostad is in unpeopled remoteness. There are cabins on the lake, many on the southeast shore, but not a soul was stirring outside on a beautiful morning.

Someone on Pelican Lake told me that the Kjostad cabin dwellers are "clannish". A few days before, on a scouting trip to find the canoe put-in site, I mistakenly went down the one-lane road that led to the cabins. I got a claustrophobic feel. People who have cabins there must be backwoodsers, so different from the open sociability of the Pelican Lake scene.

Kjostad lakeshore cabin dwellers seem to feel an "Our lake! Stay out!" possessiveness. I conclude that from the fact that one of them tore down the road sign directing to the shoreline county park and boat launch. (The earlier shotgun peppering of the sign to obliterate the lettering must not have been effective.) It took me some trial-and-error persistence to gain access. No wonder I was on the lake alone. (I imagined that the Kjostad people were eying me suspiciously through binoculars.)

But back to the Nature of Kjostad Lake:

A hunting eagle, two mergansers, and a pair of loons with a chick led me to expect excellent fishing on Kjostad Lake, but the result of my efforts did not quite satisfy such high anticipation.

Nonetheless, in any fishing you might catch the unexpected. A fish sample census of Kjostad Lake took in 291 fish, of which only one was a largemouth bass. Despite that indicative record, I caught five largemouth bass and had two more get away. I caught the bass not in the main lake, but some in a dead-end channel and some in a creek. (I guess that the largemouth bass too are clannish on Kjostad.)

I paddled a short way into that creek at the end of the northwest bay. I came across a beaver lodge there, currently occupied, as I could tell by fresh-chewed green branches and wet mud at the base. Did I hear a whimpering from within the lodge?

Continuing my circumnavigation along the north shore, I saw a stretch of sand beach, a feature uncommon in northern Minnesota lakes. I accepted the invitation and opportunity. Beaching my canoe on the sand, I shed my clothes and entered the water for a swim. I soothed my shoulder paddling muscles in the cool water.

– – –(H. L. Mencken said that "People go camping because they like to get dirty."

Mencken would have found himself contradicted if he went camping with me. In the wild I practice the same bodily hygiene I was taught as a child. That is quite easy, because there is water available all over the northland. I bathe off the sweat of exertion and any environmental dirt in a convenient lake or river. I wash myself, immerse myself, thoroughly cleanse myself.

However, privacy might sometimes be violated. One time I was just emerging from my bath in a Quetico river, when, turning, I saw three canoeloads of teenage

Girl Scouts just rounding a bend in the river and paddling towards me. Those girls got one glimpse of raw Nature that they never expected.)– – –

Now, emerging from a Kjostad Lake devoid of other people, I got dressed, then paddled over to the big island, landed the canoe, disembarked, and ate my lunch under the **NO TRESSPASSING!** sign.

I spent the day, then, in the next week, several more days getting to know Kjostad Lake. As with people, you don't perceive the full idiosyncratic uniqueness of a lake on a brief and superficial acquaintance. To get to know a lake, you have to stare hard and long into its depths over a period of time. Kjostad Lake is not just the same as the other 9,999.

\* \* \* \* \*

It is not necessary to travel far to see much. The best technique for the naturalist is to sit still in a suitable location and let Nature pass in review. (A "suitable location" is outside, not inside looking vacantly through a window. All senses must be directly exposed.)

I just step outside, walk a little way, stop, look about and listen, and I am likely to see and experience something new, something different, from what I have seen and experienced before.

Some recent examples from the nearby:

<<A flicker landed at her nest hole high in the great white pine, a tree right by my cabin, but neither flicker nor nest hole had I seen before in the probable several weeks of their presence, due to the height of the hole, far above common sight lines. It was only because

it was early morning and I happened to look up to the sunlit treetops that I saw, from my own deck, what had been there to see all along,--the flicker, her body now bright with sunlight, landing at the entrance to the nest hole.>>

<<Sitting on my observation stump on the tip of the Point one evening, I gazed across the cove. A doe emerged from the woods with her fawn. The two stepped down into the shallow water. The doe licked her fawn's flanks and back legs, giving them a vigorous cleaning. The fawn hunched up and stiffened, so as not to be pushed over by the doe's licks. Not much different from a small boy submitting to a Saturday night bath.>>

<<Just after having read how rare it is to get a good sighting observation of a pileated woodpecker—despite it being the largest North American woodpecker, now that the ivory-billed is apparently extinct—, I descended from the Point when I heard loud tree-knocking. I crept along, then squatted in the undergrowth and listened directionally. There on the bark of a birch tree broken by the wind clung the red-crested rarity, hammering away, pulling out grubs and ants. When I noticed that the sound didn't match the woodpecker's actions, I surmised what turned out to be the case. Another pileated was on the back of the tree. The hidden one soon came around to share food with the one I first saw silhouetted in profile. And so, my pileated sighting, not one, but two.>>

<<Late summer, it's already well dark at 10 o'clock. A nearly full moon competed against the star show, so, instead of looking up, I looked down, into the shallow water at the tip of the Point. I shone the flashlight among the boulders, the haunts of the lurking nightlings, the crayfish. The spotlight first fell upon a

small one in the middle of a flattop boulder. He stopped startled, but, as I held the light steady on him, he became accustomed and went on with his dining, shoving with two claws the nutritious organic debris into his mouth. I next spotlighted a large crayfish at the opening of a triangular crevice. That one backed into the rock fortress, holding two claws out forward in defense. Nearby, another one slinked down a vertical rock face. Those boulders, barren by daylight, are all acrawl with crayfish under moon and stars.>>

<<Thump. Thump. Swoosh. Thump.

The peninsula was being bombed with grenades that thumped the ground but did not explode. I made my way among the trees to investigate.

A pinecone thumped at my feet. It had not fallen by the release of ripeness, nor had it been broken off by the wind. A little furry acrobat was snipping off cones with his sharp incisors; a red squirrel working away at his late summer harvest for winter provisioning.

The squirrel detected my presence and erupted in barks, squeaks, and the wheezing of an infant's squeeze toy. All agitated now, he jumped among the boughs, then came down the trunk to the ground, as if to defend what he had acquired for himself by his treetop labors. He glared at me with his bright white-ringed eyes.

The warning having been served, he proceeded to the next pine tree, still throwing out insults and threats. Up the trunk he scooted, up to the very top. (There never was an acrophobic squirrel.)

Thump. Swoosh. Thump.>>

# The Human Presence

When I was the director of a resident summer camp for children, we would start each day with a flag ceremony in the open air, the flagpole located on the parade ground, a vast expanse of mowed grass.

After the children had been in the camp a week or more, I would wait for an overcast day, and, once the flag ceremony was completed, I would step forward and direct the children, "Everybody, point to where the sun comes up every day."

After some hesitation and a quizzical looking-around from one to another, the arms would go up and forefingers pointed...to every possible degree of bearing on a compass.

The children were bewildered. They couldn't all be right. The sun didn't rise just anywhere,—they knew that. But where was the right direction? The overcast concealed the immediate answer.

The children had been on the site for many days, some days so sunny that the children may have had to shield their eyes to lift their heads for the raising of the flag.-

Now, where did that sun come up? Didn't they know? Hadn't they experienced some sunrises there?

The children looked around in wonder at the many contradictions of their own pointed finger. They lost confidence in their answer.

They scanned the assembly. (Everyone could see everyone else, because they were formed in a large inward-facing rectangle in front of the flagpole.) Some changed their answer in imitation of what seemed to be the majority pointed direction; some argued with a neighbor who pointed elsewhere; some just dropped their hands befuddled.

They all looked to me, Nature Norm, to provide the answer with my upraised arm and pointed finger.

I kept my arms at my side.

I dismissed the assembly to the dining hall for breakfast. As we walked along, I heard the children questioning and arguing and expressing doubt.

. . . It is not only our children who fail to attain an orientation to Nature.

\* \* \* \* \*

Standing on the tip of the Point, the fishing rod in my hand.

I survey the surface of the lake. Where should I direct the cast of my lure? Where lurks the fish that I will catch?

Far to my right, a spot where I have caught some fine bass. I make an accurate cast right there.

I let the splash of the lure subside. Then I begin a slow retrieve, in expectation of a strike.

The lure chugs along the surface, drawn in toward me, I all in anticipation of a reeling-in of a fish.

By halfway back, the lure has provoked no strike. Maybe I should have used a different lure.

I continue my retrieve, now thinking about the next spot I will cast to.

My concentration is distracted. Even as the lure still comes along, I am considering a different lure and a different spot, a better spot, one where I will catch a fish.

The lure brought in, no fish on the line, I make a cast to that next spot.

Once again, as my lure is halfway back, I consider whether I should have used a different lure and whether I should cast to yet some other spot.

And maybe this is the wrong time to be fishing. Maybe at dusk would be better.

On through my whole session of fishing, casting to one spot after another, unsuccessful at the halfway point of the retrieve, I am already thinking about a different lure, the better spot to cast to, and about maybe giving up now and coming back later....

That is the process of our mind all through our life: While doing one thing, we think of doing some other thing, we think of some other place, and something possibly better to come. We take ourselves out of this-here-now by imagining prospects of something-else, somewhere-else, some-other-time. No wonder we fail to catch any fish.

* * * * *

## The Human Presence

I was hiking the Vermilion Gorge Trail, when I saw a side path descending toward the river. Wanting to get down to the river, as well as look down upon it, I followed the descent to the water's edge.

As I stood on the riverbank, a motorboat approached, idling along in the flowage, parallel to, and not far off, the bank.

One person was in the boat, the man at the wheel.

Despite the fact that I was in clear exposed view and wearing a bright blue nylon jacket besides, the man did not see me.

Unobserved, I observed.

The man's head was down, as he drove the boat past me. I saw a cell-phone pressed to his ear and heard his voice. He was evidently concentrating on his phone conversation.

He went by me down the length of the flow, his head always down. I thought he must glance up now and then to direct his course, but, as he was going so slowly and there being few other boats around, he didn't mind his steering.

He never once looked up at the cascading tapestry of woods along the river.

At last, he lowered the cell-phone from his ear.

Then he searched for a paper on his dashboard, dialed a new number and, head down still, began another phone conversation.

Some people here are not here.

\* \* \* \* \*

While I was canoeing from the Pelican River to Rice Lake, the diesel roar and the hammering of the machines of the railroad bridge repair crew intruded a sonic dissonance.

There was also a dissonance imposed upon my eyes. Beyond the far end of Rice Lake I saw several cell-phone and other communication towers, the height of which was double that of the tree line.

I shouldn't editorialize against cell-phone towers, because I have a cell-phone in my cabin. I am not against human communication. What I can't stand is all the empty yackety-yack and the private trivia spilled out in public places. Also, I've seen the cell-phone towers every five miles the entire north-south extent of the state of Illinois. The most conspicuous surface feature, they dominate the landscape. (Subject to change; the wind turbine farms are springing up everywhere.)

- - - NEWS FLASH! A LAWSUIT HAS JUST BEEN FILED TO PREVENT THE ERECTION OF A CELL-PHONE TOWER OVERLOOKING THE BOUNDARY WATERS CANOE AREA WILDERNESS. WILDERNESS VALUES WILL BE THREATENED BY THE TOWER, ENVIRONMENTALISTS CLAIM. - - -

But how can we expect our hardy, roughin'-it adventurer to leave behind what he says he is escaping from?

An argument for the cell-phone tower overlooking the Boundary Waters is safety. What if some adventurer suffers a health emergency or mishap of accident? Cell-phone use availability will enable quick medical evacuation.

Yes, we should do what we can to reduce risk, but let's keep in mind that cell-phone technology has caused hundreds of automobile drivers to talk their way into horrific crashes. Whether cell-phones cause brain cancer is an open question; cell-phone caused car crackups is not. We have to lay the record of irresponsibility against any proposed benefit to a rare situation of wilderness emergency. Now will we have chatterboxes tumbling out of canoes?

An AT&T spokesman was recently in Ely, talking up proposed 4G broadband service. "What it means," he said, "is that Ely is no different than downtown Minneapolis, no different than downtown St. Paul."

If so, let's put an end to the obsolete association of the words *Ely* and *wilderness*.

AT&T promises that, if it succeeds in acquiring T-Mobile USA, 99% of Minnesotans will have access to wireless broadband.

Pity the unfortunate 1%, deprived of high-speed communication. They'll have to remain old-fashioned low-speed face-to-face talkers.

A son of a neighbor of mine (no tech-crazed teenager he, but a middle-aged man), seeing me on my way to my cabin yesterday, pursued me and asked, "Do you have Wi-Fi in your cabin?"

His question was in a tone of pleading, pathetic urgency.

"I can't get along without Wi-Fi," he explained.

"Wi-Fi? Who, me?" I answered. "I don't even have a television in my cabin."

"I have a radio," I added in self-justification.

Thoreau said that they could run a telegraph line from Maine to Texas, but what if Maine had nothing to say to Texas? The business goal of the telephone and Internet companies is everybody talking all the time or everybody online all the time, maximizing revenue for the service providers. The significance, value, or meaning of the communication is of no interest.

A duck's quacking has meaning, but a duck shuts up once in a while.

The wilderness should be the last refuge from the babelous violations of peace-and-quiet and the compulsive connectedness to electronic sensations. The racket of communication is deafening. Instead of communication, I want to commune. Communing with Nature is a one-way listening, even if only to the sacred silence.

* * * * *

Why go into the woods, into any wild, at all?

I found some answers to that challenging question when I spent a week on a solo canoeing/camping excursion into the Boundary Waters.

My outfitter surprised me by trying to dissuade me from going solo, even though he knew me as an experienced and competent *voyageur*.

"Go by yourself?" he asked. What if you break your leg or something?"

"I'll still have two good arms," I answered. "I'll be able to paddle over to the First Nation village for help."

"By yourself, you might go bushwhacky."

(*Bushwhacky* means stir-crazy.)

"I think I can stand myself for a week," I answered.

To go into the wild is to incur risk. To get up every morning is to incur risk. Despite my outfitter's double apprehension on my behalf—(concern for the welfare of both my body and my mind)—, I had no reason to believe that the risks of the wild are any more fearsome than the risks of modern civilized life.

The residents of my town in suburban Chicago have become all apprehensive over coyotes that have been making incursions into town. However, hospital records reveal that, in a typical year, about 900 people in the county are bitten by dogs; there hasn't been a single coyote bite. The reality of risk can be very different from the perception of risk.

As for my going solo, I had already had the experiences of going into the wild as a member of a large group, as a foursome, and as a twosome. What I learned was, the more people, the less immersion in the environment. The presence of a lot of people around you creates a primarily social experience, no matter where you are. Solo would be I-in-Nature, the most basic, most direct, relatedness. Regarding any risk involved, the likelihood of an accident is lowest when you are fully concentrated on what you are doing, without the distraction of other people. Just consider a teenager driving a car full of other teenagers.

Besides risk, another objection to going into the wild is hardship. Isn't the whole point of civilization a making-it-easier for ourselves? Hasn't all human effort been directed toward leaving primitive subsistence living behind?

I once heard an interviewer asking a woodsman old-timer about roughing-it. "Roughing-it?" the woodsman corrected the interviewer. "I don't rough it. I smooth it."

I have nothing in common with yahoo thrill seekers to whom the environment is the adversary, who take to the wild to prove their manhood by plunging themselves into all sorts of risks in the name of *adventure*. As another old-timer said, "Adventure is what happens to the incompetent."

To go into the wild intelligently is to get down to the basics without self-inflicted hardships or damnfool recklessness. Feeding oneself is one basic. If I catch the fish that will be my evening meal, then modern man attains at least a modicum of self-sufficiency.

A first reason for going into the wild is to get *out*. We don't realize the stifling interiority of the lives we lead. Car, cubicle, room, office, shop, indoor mall, house, apartment,—we spend the most of our lives inside, secure, comfortable, yes, but stifled too.

The indoors life is one of sensory privation. To go out into Nature is to re-awaken as the animal, organic creatures that we are. Animal sensoriness is where life throbs in us. To breathe deeply of wholesome air, to feel the weather on the skin, to look hard, to listen intently, to be fully aware,—that is what it is to be alive.

How pathetic, by contrast, is the sensory privation of our electronic communication and entertainment. When I first saw a man with the little rectangular device attached to his ear, I assumed a hearing-aid, but, no, it was a phone, he ready to instantly respond to any ringing, like Pavlov's dogs. People walk around talking to no one there. The nonstop self-inflicted distractions of our electronics would make us all nervous wrecks. How therapeutic the silence of the wild!

I told the outfitter that I would go into the wild, and go there solo.

He dropped me off on an island with canoe, camping gear, and basic supplies. I paddled, portaged, and set up camp on the shore of a small lake. Solo, but well companioned by the Nature around me. I spent a safe and easy week.

What I found myself satisfying on my solo excursion was not so much my need for Nature as the needs of my own human nature. The enervating distractions left behind, I could live the concentrated life, elemental in my attention to food, clothing, and shelter, attentive in my carrying-out of campsite tasks, alert and aware of my surroundings, relaxed and receptive to the world as it presented itself, feeling my place in that world, enjoying health and vitality. In all, a most wholesome experience. I underwent a physiological and psychological restoration.

Physiological, psychological, and spiritual too. The spirituality to be found in the natural is *attunement*, the concentrated awareness of belonging and participation in our world of life. Sitting still in the woods or drifting on the lake in my canoe, I tuned in.

To go into the wild is not really to escape anything. It is to return and rediscover.

*****

I have built many campfires over the years, some for cooking, some for warmth, some for atmosphere. Looking back, I don't think a campfire was the best means to those ends.

Using a campfire to cook food is a protracted process. Starting a fire in the north woods is easy; birch bark is highly flammable. But fuel to sustain the fire may be scarce or unsuitable. Heavily used campsites are usually depleted of good downed timber; what remains is often rotten. Then too, in rainy periods all the wood may be wet. A fire must be carefully constructed and constantly tended to attain the exact height of flame or heat of coals needed for the particular food being prepared. Handling pots and utensils around a fire is awkward, what with dancing flames and swirling smoke. In all, a campfire is a rigmarole to the satisfaction of hunger.

Early on, I switched to a Coleman camp stove for cooking. Instant flame, a quick hot meal. I was especially glad of the stove when I happened to arrive at a take-off point and was informed that, due to drought conditions, open fires had been banned throughout the Boundary Waters.

As for warmth, I recall a remark Chief Wa-wa-tay-see once made to me: "The white man builds a big fire and sits far away. The red man builds a small fire and sits near." Yes, a big fire is extra work for no added benefit.

The human body is best warmed by radiant heat. The flames of a campfire, shooting straight up, are not radiant. If you extend your cold fingertips too close to the flames, you will feel singed. Back off and you're in the cold again. Coals are radiant, but they take a long time to achieve. Meanwhile, you stand by shivering.

Some have advocated heating rocks in a campfire, then putting those heated rocks at the foot of the sleeping bag. I have heard of rocks that, heated in a fire, actually explode. I don't know whether Minnesota has that type of rock, but, even if it doesn't, I don't want to scorch the sleeping bag. For warmth, I would just as soon forget the fire and climb directly into the sleeping bag.

Campfires may be used to dry wet clothes, but attempting that might just render the clothes smoky and still soggy. You'd be better off looking for a sun-warmed black rock surface upon which to lay the wet clothes, or else hang the clothes from a limb to dry in the northland breezes.

When I was a camp director, one of the traditions of the camp was the construction of a bonfire, ten or twelve feet high, to be set alight during nighttime ceremonials. The flaming tower was an impressive sight to children's eyes, but the effect of a bonfire is an arousal of pyromania.

The campfire has also served as a focal setting for group camaraderie, with the charred marshmallow the eucharist of woodland fellowship. In these days of video games, Internet, and the many other forms of electronic isolation, however, the "Let's all gather 'round the campfire" is an invitation that will receive no response.

The campfire does hearken back to the primordial experience of the human species. I have seen visions in the flames or the glowing coals.

A campfire may create a nostalgic, romantic aura for the outdoors experience. That aura, however, can turn blinding and choking. Even though I am seated upwind of my small fire, the capricious wind turns and swirls smoke over me. I move and the smoke follows. Later, my hair and clothes reek of wood smoke. I become a smudge pot, like a cigarette smoker. The lingering stench of smoke muffles my sensitivity to the natural scents and fragrances of the north woods.

Considering all this, I've come to regard a campfire—except in real cold or in desperate survival situations—as just so much more air pollution.

\* \* \* \* \*

Most people in our contemporary United States are urbanites or suburbanites, whose lives are lit up by night as by day, electricity substituting when the sun has departed to bestow his illuminative favors on the other side of the planet.

We make our own light at night, whether within our houses when we settle in, or in the streets for nocturnal pedestrians, or headlight beams if we want to drive off in the night from one lit place to another.

A householder needs lit bulbs as he makes his way to the kitchen for a midnight snack, but how to explain his yard light when no one is outside? For security, or at least a sense of security. I suppose primitive men added fuel to the campfire and stoked it before lying down to sleep close to the light.

Some of our nocturnal artificial lighting seems senseless, like the hundreds of lit-up office windows in a skyscraper whose office workers have all gone home hours ago. That night lighting—the entire nighttime cityscape, in fact—is a show and a show-off.

We humans have evolved with poor night vision, but, when it gets naturally dark, we won't go off to bed, as we should.

In my role as Nature Norm, I used to take children on night hikes. They would all show up with a flashlight, ostensibly to light the way ahead. In talking and interacting, however, they would shine their flashlights at one another, even into one another's eyes. Then came a waving of flashlights for a beacon effect, light-saber dueling, and so much competitive light show as to blind everybody.

The next time, I told them, "No flashlights!" "But how can we see anything?" they protested. "The stars and full moon will light the way for you," I promised and assured. I told them that I myself would carry a flashlight, but I would turn it on only at an emergency.

The children were reluctant to venture forth into the night without artificial lighting. They were skeptical of the adequacy of stars and moon, and they were afraid of unseen dangers lurking. Yet, once their eyes became accustomed to the natural light of night and the emerging stars and constellations gradually revealed themselves, what a wonder the children saw! On one particular night, there was even a spectacular display of the aurora borealis, very rare in southern Wisconsin. At that event, the children experienced what can only be described as enlightenment.

Here on Pelican Lake, the sun illumines land and water from sunrise to sunset. North woods and natural Nature that this area supposedly is, at dusk the electric lights come on. From my canoe in the middle of the lake, I see a shoreline of lights,—lights of utility, of security, of show and show-off, every burning bulb an assertion of human technological will and a rebuttal of the natural.

In city and suburb, there are so many ground lights that it is impossible to see the full epiphany of the starlit night. Due to all the light pollution around them, 80% of Americans cannot even see the very conspicuous Milky Way.

The lights on my Westmont neighbor's garage are so bright and shine through my bedroom window with such intensity that, until I installed a heavy-gauge vinyl opaque shade, I couldn't get to sleep, my shut eyelids an insufficient screen. There would be no point in attempting a star hike in my well-lit, overlit, suburban neighborhood.

The artificial nightlights hereabouts on Pelican Lake are fewer, somewhat scattered, and, so, less overpowering. From the Point, I have the opportunity to experience a celestial vision of the astral splendor of the infinite firmament.

*****

Many of those who flee city, town, or suburb to the north woods proceed to transform the north woods by imposing the environment of city, town, or suburb. They cut down trees, build—overbuild—a pseudo-rustic megacabin and surround it with a planted grass lawn and garden ornaments (plastic deer in a land of live deer). Garages, pole buildings, and sheds hold all the machines they have dragged along with them. A TV satellite dish, and all is then perfect for living in the woods.

The purchaser of a patch of north woods surveys his acquired domain. Too many trees obstructing free movement, too much undergrowth underfoot. And so, he wields chain-saw, shovel, and weed whacker. Finding two trees at the right distance for a hammock, he spares them. They serve him and his reconstructive vision.

A lady called in a logger to cut down a robust, healthy pine tree so that she might have a level broad stump for a flowerpot.

People want an environment as the setting for their personal idiosyncratic lives. Not the human in the environment-as-it-is, but the environment recast and made suitable to human domestic life. What people value is not the natural integrity of a place, but the scenic possibilities conceived by human whim. Nature is just scenery to look upon when the TV is off.

My cabin is right on the shoreline of Pelican Lake. Between the cabin and the lake is a characteristic native stand of birches and balsams. I've been asked why I don't cut down some of the trees to open up my view of the lake. But shall my view be of other's open views? The lake doesn't want a better look at me.

The last thing I would ever consider doing here is mowing a lawn. This is the boreal forest, floor of pine, spruce, and balsam needles, just as it should be.

A man down the road has purchased an adjacent homestead in order to give himself a farther distance from any neighbor. He demolished all the structures on the purchased property. As I walked by, I saw the heaps of building debris, the wreckage of what was for many years a human habitation. The mobile home had been pulled off the property to the roadside for hauling away. Through the gap where the door once was, I looked upon the rusted appliances and the dated wallpaper, a sepia woodland scene of deer and ducks. Fiberglass insulation hung out of holes in the mobile home frame. All was obsolescence and dilapidation.

I don't think that any human construction is an improvement upon the landscape. It is, rather, disfigurement and squalor, even when new.

Huge A-frame cabins with more window glass than wall (for the insulated view) are erected on high bluffs. A manicured lawn slopes down to the shoreline, a few trees left for woodsiness, but not so many as to kill off the grass by too much shade. A boathouse stands on the shore, piers with moored motorboats project out into the lake. Land and water both made serviceable.

We can make it all better with a little investment and a general tidying-up. And all fenced in to indicate *my-own*.

What if we could turn the north woods into a golf course? Or at least a picnic park.

*The Human Presence*

The north woods, the best, most scenic, place to be. Ah, Nature!

\* \* \* \* \*

I came across a real estate ad for a "stunning Burntside estate", the lead selling point of which was that "Sigurd Olson's Listening Point is just down the bay."

Sigurd Olson, our northland naturalist, a Minnesotan long resident on Burntside Lake near Ely. Gone now, but, for advertising purposes at least, not forgotten.

The "Listening Point" referred to was to Sigurd Olson what my own Point on Pelican Lake is to me. *Listening Point* was the title of one of Olson's many books about Nature and the wilderness.

Associating Sigurd Olson with property to be bought reminds me of a sign I saw in Concord, Massachusetts. "Thoreau Realty", it said. A real estate office named after a man who warned against buying and owning property. Owned land was an encumbrance, according to Thoreau. You could experience all that land offers without owning any. (As for a possible family descent relationship as an explanation for the sign, I ruled that out. The immediate family of Henry David Thoreau went extinct.)

Back to the Coldwell Banker ad and to Sigurd Olson:—

The *estate* on Burntside Lake is 5.4 acres, with 205 feet of lakeshore. More yet, the house is 13,000 square feet. With such spaciousness of domicile, who would need an expanse of Nature outside?

The manor house is fronted by a deck with "big water views". I don't think that looking at water hour after hour will compete with the visual extravaganzas to be enjoyed in the house's very own cinema.

And how about time in the pool, or by the pool with a glass of wine from the wine cellar? There's plenty of water in Burntside Lake for swimming, but I suspect that the water of Burntside Lake has that Minnesota chill to it, definitely a deterrent to all but the hardy. The ad doesn't specify whether the pool is outside or inside; I think the latter, for what would be the advantage otherwise? Cold air overlies cold outdoor water in our dear Minnesota.

The property is a "short ride to historic Burntside Lodge". I don't know whether any prospective buyer has ever heard of the Lodge, but anyway, that promises a social escape from the boredom of 5.4-acre-encompassing isolation. No need to trudge out, either; other people are just a short car ride away. The place is so imposing that the residents will have to get away from it.

And the listening of "Listening Point"? The ad promises "soothing sounds of cascading waterfalls & wind in the towering pines". Yes, the flow of water is a pleasant music. The ad writer shouldn't have mentioned the wind, however. Around my cabin the *derecho* has laid low many pines; they tower no more. The terrifying crashes of wind destruction are a northwoods unpleasantness.

Curiously, the ad urges the property as a hospitable place to "relax and entertain".

A possible reaction: "We're invited to where? What, where the hell is that? Mosquitoes and bats...I hope it's not any outdoor barbeque...."

I'd reassure the invited guests with talk of the built-in cinema, the pool, and the wine cellar. The words "formal dining" in the ad are reassuring, too.

The estate offers "wilderness with every amenity".

What?! There are no amenities in the wilderness. That's what *wilderness* means.

"Listening Point." Listening to what? And what's the point?

* * * * *

The resort closest to my own cabin invites prospective guests to "Make tracks to one of the finest family resorts in northern Minnesota".

In order to make tracks, you have to walk. I've never seen a guest of the resort arrive by walking. They all motor in.

What are the attractions of the resort? Their advertisement lists them: Heated Pool. Hot Tub. Wireless Internet. Satellite TV. Air Conditioning.

"All in a wilderness setting."

Huh?

The resort offers not cabins but "new log vacation accommodations".

By the way, those accommodations run $1,000 to $2,000 rental per week. Gee, the wilderness has certainly gotten costly.

Richer living than that in the forest hovels of Henry David Thoreau, Sigurd Olson, and Nature Norm, isn't it?

\* \* \* \* \*

I was drawn into a casual conversation with a fellow who soon turned the casual into the concentrated, for there was something on his mind that was sorely bothering him. He disburdened himself upon me, a bystander and stranger.

The fellow is a property owner on the shoreline of a nearby lake. One of his neighbors, he said, decided to challenge the existing property lines. The neighbor commissioned a resurvey, which discovered an error of 100 feet in the existing lines of the adjacent shoreline properties. He then took legal action to enforce the adjustment.

The property holders there, some of them, had been secure on the site for 20 or 30 years. You can imagine the disruption and dismay caused by the resurvey. There was subsequent litigation, of course, especially by those most adversely affected.

Each person was dispossessed of 100 feet at one end of his property and now possessed of 100 feet of what had been his neighbor's on the other end. One person lost his stand of tall red pines and acquired scrub. Another lost his level lake frontage and acquired a boulder pile. A newly drawn property line went right through someone's shed. The fellow complaining to me said that the gravel approach road to his cabin was now on the neighbor's property, and his expanse now broken by a rock cliff.

You would think that the courts would let *de facto* possession alone, especially 30 years' worth, but, no, the court ordered the long-ago error rectified by redrawing property lines, never mind that that would set previously amicable neighbors at one another's throats.

My conversational complainant told me that he wanted to take his appeal all the way to the Minnesota Supreme Court, but he lacked the financial means to do so. He had paid taxes on his land all those years, he said; didn't that entitle him to secure permanent ownership?

He complained bitterly that the person who benefited most from the redrawn lines was the one who initiated the resurvey. That one happened to be a public official; "the fix was in," the complainant alleged.

"Well, I got over it," the dispossessed fellow said, even as the intensity with which he told the story, the doggedness with which he always returned to the issue when I tried to change the subject, the repetition of not only the entire story but all the details,—all indicated that he was not over it, but, rather, was held in the grip of a grievance obsession.

Ownership of land, private property,—a fine notion to set people against one another.

The 100-foot dislocation had no effect upon the rocks and trees, but what an effect upon the human mind and emotions!

The Native Americans believed that we belong to the land, not vice-versa. We disabused the Indians of that naive sentimentality by dispossessing them of North America, which we then checkerboarded with property lines.

Looking from my cabin across Susan Bay at the panorama of woods on the shore, I see no straight lines of demarcation and division. In Nature, there is no concept of property. Property is a legal fiction possessing the human mind. Property owns us.

Every individual organism in Nature needs its living space, of course. Some animals are territorial in relation to others of their own species, but only the human exercises the right of exclusion by privatizing the entire landscape.

I pray God that no resurvey pushes my cabin and me in it off my peninsula, down the slope of the Point, and into the bottom of Pelican Lake.

* * * * *

When my nephew was a boy, I asked him what he wanted to be when he grew up.

"I want to be a game warden," he said.

I thought that a peculiar ambition for a boy living in suburbia.

"A game warden? Why?"

"I want to shoot poachers," my nephew answered.

I considered that a bit, then told my nephew that if he wanted to save the animals, instead of shooting poachers, he should shoot property developers.

I then explained that poachers kill individual animals, but property developers destroy the environment within which the species tries to survive. Destroying an environment dooms the future of many species that live there.

I told my nephew that his neighborhood and the town itself—all houses and schools and churches, office buildings and shopping malls, and paved streets and driveways—was once a forest. That forest is now gone, along with many of the creatures that lived within it. The perpetrator of that crime against Nature was not the poaching hunter, but the real estate speculator and the property developer.

Animals displaced are on their way to ultimate disappearance.

It is not only urbanization that displaces the denizens of Nature. Rural America is just as thorough. When I was a boy spending my summers on a farm, it was common for crop fields to be surrounded by hedgerows that marked property lines or served as windbreaks. Those hedgerows provided some shelter and refuge for birds and rabbits. Farming today, however, is edge-to-edge intensive, hedgerows all gone, agricultural land just a vast barren emptiness waiting to be exclusively occupied by next year's crop.

(In further conversation I perceived that my nephew's attraction to a career as a game warden had more to do with its lawman aspect than with its role in conservation.)

Yes, poaching must be prevented or punished, in order to preserve the game. (*Game* means an animal meant to be killed, but with such limitations as to ensure a future supply of animals to be killed.)

Stanley, an old fishing buddy of mine, used to regale me with tales of fantastic fish abundance in the remote lakes of the northland back in the 1930s. No more, he said. Roads since cut through to those lakes, as well as easy accessibility by floatplane, have depleted the lakes by overfishing.

"It's just greed, damn greed," Stanley said. "If everyone took out only what they needed, everything would be OK. But some guys want to take it all for themselves. Damn greed!"

One day, when I brought in a small pike for my dinner, an old-timer said to me, "Is that all you caught? Why, we used to fill the boat with big pike any time we wanted them. Why can't you do that?"

"We can't do it, because of what you guys once did," I told him in the tone of Stanley's indictment. The old-timer bristled and scowled at me.

Since people lack self-restraint to stop at enough, there must be rules and regulations, enforced by the game wardens and the courts.

The current brochure of *Minnesota Fishing Regulations* is 92 pages, a deep read! On page 22, I discover that the legal 23" northern pike I caught and ate last summer has become illegal this summer, illegal by one inch. So the continuous fine tuning of the regulations. In trying to keep up, I study the 92 pages and memorize the range of inches before I pocket a tape measure and then dare to put baited line into the water.

The goal of it all is *management* of the *renewable resource*, the fishery of Minnesota. What with scientific research, fish surveys, fish hatcheries and stocking, administration and enforcement, such management must pay its expenses.

Fishing licenses provide the needed revenue. The more management, the more expensive licenses have become. $68 is now the cost for my wife and myself to fish for our bluegill dinner out of Pelican Lake.

I sometimes wonder whether the high cost of fishing licenses might have the perverse effect of actually inducing fishermen to take and keep more fish than they otherwise would, in order to feel that they are getting their money's worth.

The back cover of the *Minnesota Fishing Regulations* brochure urges, "TURN IN THE POACHERS" and provides a 24-hour hotline to do so. To whom can I report the assaults upon the natural environment perpetrated by the real estate speculators and the property developers?

* * * * *

The *boundary* of the Boundary Waters is that between the state of Minnesota and the province of Ontario, or, more broadly, that between the United States and Canada.

We think of a boundary as a fixed straight line, but the boundary of the Boundary Waters is a most fluid and meandering one; it runs right down the middle of a chain of lakes and rivers. In the waters of my familiar canoeing excursions, the international boundary (I might say) *flows through* Lac La Croix, the Loon River, Crane Lake, Sandpoint Lake, Namakan Lake, and Rainy Lake.

Canada is north of the United States, mostly, that is. When I am canoeing on Namakan Lake, depending on where I happen to be on that lake, Canada may lie to the north, to the east, or even to the south. The lakes in the chain link up every which direction, to the frustration of the makers of boundaries, those lovers of the straight line.

Further to the confusion of the international boundary is a peninsula in Lake of the Woods known as the Northwest Angle. It belongs to the United States. An American can boat over to it, but, if he is in his car, he must have passport in hand as he drives through the province of Manitoba to get to that piece of stranded United States territory.

Just as a private property deed imposes no restriction upon the sprawl of Nature, so nation-state claims of land or water, asserted by an international boundary line, are an empty distinction to a naturalist, who identifies the fish in Namakan Lake by species, not by citizenship.

Fishermen, however, carry their citizenship in the boat with them. If an American with no passport and a Minnesota fishing license inadvertently fishes in a Namakan bay that is actually on the Canadian side of the invisible line on the water, he becomes an illegal alien illegally fishing. If he happens to have in his live well fish caught on the American side, an Ontario warden will consider those fish caught in Canada, compounding the violation. A Canadian with no passport and only an Ontario license fishing inadvertently on American-claimed Namakan offends vice-versa.

Once, on a day of strenuous canoeing, I pulled up to a rock pile in the middle of a Boundary Waters lake and got out to stretch and relax.

I discovered, driven into the rock, an obelisk about two feet tall. Not a haphazard glacial deposit that stone spire, but a manmade object.

I knelt down to examine my find. I saw a medallion seal, *United States Geological Survey.* One face of the obelisk read *United States*; the opposite face read *Canada*.

Well, there it was, an exact point on the dividing line between two nation-states.

I stood over the marker and spread my legs, so that my left foot was planted in the United States, my right foot firmly in Canada. Remarkable! I was in two countries at the same time.

But now what? If I lifted my left foot, I was entered into Canada illegally, without passport. If I then put left foot down and lifted my right foot, I would have re-entered the United States without going through a citizenship check or Customs.

I leapt back into my canoe and swiftly paddled off to I-knew-not-where. An international fugitive making an escape!

\* \* \* \* \*

"We are still here."

Those words are addressed to a society that may think them a people past and gone.

The vast north woods had once been their domain. Invaders displaced them and confined them to circumscribed tracts, mere parcels, like the Nett Lake Reservation and the Vermilion Lake Reservation. Out of sight, out of mind.

Still here, they are the Ojibwe, the ones the invaders called the Chippewa, but they themselves the *Anishinaabeg*, the original people (the aboriginal).

The displacement inflicted upon the Ojibwe was not only physical; it was cultural too. Ojibwe children were take away from their parents, stripped of their tribal garb, suited with starched shirt-and-tie, forced to learn and speak only English, and inculcated with patriotism to the United States and belief in Baptist Christianity. Such imperialistic education deformed several generations of Ojibwe.

The Ojibwe adults too were treated like children. Chiefdom, the elders, and councils of tribal self-government were subjected to the authoritarian oversight of Indian agents.

How could the Ojibwe keep their traditional way-of-life? Their northwoods economy of free-moving hunting, trapping, gathering, and fishing could not continue in a society of boundaries and private property barriers.

The Ojibwe people and their way-of-life became obsolete in what was now the modern world of nation state, urbanism, and technosphere.

A people stripped of their culture is a people lost, even if not gone. The Ojibwe world, the world to which they belonged, had become an alien environment controlled by domineering aliens.

The consequences of the treatment of the Ojibwe were the familiar pathologies of the Native American,— alcoholism, drug addiction, domestic violence, family disintegration, unemployment, and suicides.

The Ojibwe have been trying to hold their own, fighting for tribal rights, drawing their children back into learning their language and culture, bolstering morale, and, as in the Bois Forte Heritage Center in Tower, Minnesota, displaying their pride as a people and educating the whites to Ojibwe identity.

At that same site in Tower, the tribally owned Fortune Bay Casino enables the Ojibwe to succeed in a little take-back. The casino sucks money out of the whites who have taken so much from the Ojibwe.

The Ojibwe know that still being here is not enough. They have survived. The ongoing challenge is to continue to be what they are in a country that doesn't acknowledge their existence.

\* \* \* \* \*

Some others who are here, still here, and must remain here are the residents of Leiding Cemetery.

The cemetery of Leiding Township is on a gently sloping hill. The tall red pines and the clumps of birches are characteristically north woods, but they are widely spaced on the mowed grass lawn of the typical cemetery scene that could be anywhere.

The grave markers are stones both flat and upright. I found no nineteenth-century graves, but some had been there long enough for the stone to be encrusted with lichens, just like the glacial boulders on the shore of Pelican Lake. The markers are modest in size and elemental in material; no indication of any affluence of those interred there in Leiding Cemetery.

The inscriptions on the grave markers record the simple basic descriptors of a human life:—the name, dates of birth and death, familial role as mother, father, daughter, son.

A few of the better gravestones feature incised artwork, as, for example, a cabin-in-the-woods scene. One stone has sketches of an accordion and banjo, another of a dancing couple, both personalizations more so than just the name. A small dog statue might be a representation of the deceased's pet, now a companion at the soul's side for all eternity.

Most cemeteries prohibit any decoration of the grave site as an obstacle to mowing. Leiding is lax in that regard. Leiding Cemetery is a garden of plastic flowers. There are also Virgin statues and shrines, standing angels, American flags, and plaques of military service. One grave is crowned by a wreath of a planted patch of lilies that annually blooms to shame the plastic flowers.

The family names of those buried in Leiding are quite familiar to anyone acquainted with the Orr area. Those names can also be found on the local roads and the stores operated by a later generation of the family.

Many of the immigrants who came to northern Minnesota were northern Europeans who shunned the teeming slums of New York in favor of the hard rigors in the north woods of North America, so similar to the environment they had left behind. From Scandinavia to Minnesota, a transposition but not an environmental dislocation.

The ethnic makeup of the families represented in Leiding Cemetery is a necropolis community of Finns, Norwegians, and Swedes: Rahikainen, Laakkonen, and Takkunen. Hanskala, Heikkila, and Toivola. Erickson, Olson, and Nelson.

Some place names in northern Minnesota record that heritage. There is the town of Finland (named in nostalgia), Norway Point, which is just down the shoreline from my cabin, and also Chisholm, Lutsen, Knutsen, and Fredenberg.

The most prominent memorial in Leiding Cemetery bears the inscription: "In memory of lumberjacks who lie in unmarked graves, 1925-1975", followed by 20 names and topped by an incised sketch of a lumberjack holding a double-bladed axe. Poignant is the reflection that those men had been buried in anonymity, poor loners lacking the deep family ties so prominent in the rest of Leiding Cemetery.

While I was wandering and musing among the graves, a man drove up in a pickup truck. He came across the road, knelt at a grave, pulled some weeds, and smoothed away the windblown pine needles and the dry grass. And so, the ongoing family ties, those with the living, as well as with the dead kin lying side-by-side in the pleasant quiet of Leiding Cemetery.

* * * * *

The creatures of the wild have had to become accustomed to the presence of the human, for the human is omnipresent.

The human, as a large upright animal, provokes fright and fear in many smaller creatures, but, with the human present at every turn, where could the other creatures flee to? The human always there, the animals have to cope with fright and fear.

There used to be a sharp distinction between wild animals in the wilderness on the one hand and farm or domestic (human associating) animals on the other. Yet, today polar bears stroll down the main street in Churchill, Manitoba and coyotes trot down Michigan Avenue in Chicago.

The loon is a bird of the northland wild, once so intolerant of human presence that a pair would abandon their nest if a human approached or was even seen. These days, loons attempt parentage here on Pelican Lake, where motorboats filled with shouting humans roar past in heavy crisscross traffic.

I remember that, when I lived in Wisconsin in the 1970s, I would see and hear on a fall migration day a great V of honking Canada geese flying overhead. Their honking was the very "call of the wild" to me. It made the hair stand up on the back of my neck in thrill, and it aroused an aching wanderlust for the wilderness.

Today, four blocks from my house in a suburb of Chicago, so many Canada geese, now become resident grazers of mowed lawn, infest our neighborhood park year-round that I have renamed the site Goosepoop Park.

The Canada goose, once clarion-caller of the wild, is now as domestic as the pigeon, and as foul a nuisance too.

Much of what was once the wilderness is now *recreational property*, where deer get run down by automobiles and bears get shot for being tempted by their hunger to frequent the trash dump, backyard garbage cans, or, worse, invade a cabin. The human encroachment upon the wilderness has some dire consequences for the denizens of the formerly wild.

Some creatures, like the grizzly bear, show a truculent, stubborn stand-tough, but, if they are to avoid extermination, they have to repress resistance, adapt, and recede.

Being deprived of some of their food by human hunters, the once wild may turn to scavenging what the human disposes of or perhaps rely on sentimental humans to now and then toss a handout.

If there is any conflict between the human and wild creatures, there is no doubt about which will triumph and which will perish.

So, we among the wild creatures, as those like me with a cabin in the woods exemplify. And the wild creatures among us, as yesterday the woebegone chipmunk dodging traffic on the hot pavement in Orr, a mere village pedestrian.

We humans complain about bird droppings on the lawn furniture or a squirrel in the attic, but, really, the heavy impact is from us upon other creatures.

Not only the human animal itself—loud, aggressive, tromping trespasser—, but all the godawful disturbers of natural peace-and-quiet that are the machines of the human,—airplanes, trains, trucks and cars, the lawn tractor, the lawn mower, the leaf blower-vac, the hedge trimmer, the snow blower (and the snowmobile!), the chain-saw, the log splitter, the generator, the compressor, on and on, an endless bedlam of noisy, even deafening machines. How do the poor besieged and battered creatures, without recourse to earplugs, stand it all?

The worst machine here on Pelican Lake is the motorboat. Look out, pelicans! Flee with your fledglings, ducks and loons! Here roars by another speedboat. My own sleep is ended at 5 a.m., when a motorboat bearing fishermen throttles out of the resort and surges past the shoreline under my cabin. Motorboat fishermen terrify and scatter more fish than they ever catch, rip up the weed beds, pollute the water with combustion effluent, toss trash overboard, and generally wreak havoc on the aquatic environment. The motorboats cause more waves to crash upon the shore than do the winds of Nature. With prop-generated swell after swell, the fish in the shallows must get seasick. Needless to say, the motorboaters do not linger to admire the garden of blue flag iris blooming in beauty along the Pelican Lake shoreline.

I once considered as a literary project an apocalyptic called, *A Requiem for Nature*. The wild is almost gone, but Nature endures, even if it is a Nature ever more contracted and dominated by the inescapable, ubiquitous impact of the human. Nature will just have to adapt, all her creatures lying low and hiding out, if the Requiem is to be postponed.

* * * * *

Pelican Lake is a cold soup into which random ingredients are being tossed.

Some of those ingredients are out of the air, dropped in by gravity. Strontium-90 from the atomic tests, volcanic ash from the eruption of Mt. St. Helens, mercury from the faraway processing of gold, rain and snow acidified by distant smokestacks, and even contaminated Chinese dirt blown across the Pacific by dust storms may all have fallen into the bowl of Pelican Lake.

If a new aquatic plant or live creature is discovered as an unwelcome addition to a lake, blame has sometimes been laid upon ducks. Paddling around in one lake, picking up seeds or eggs on its feet or feathers, that duck may then fly off to another lake, drop in, and release those seeds or eggs there.

Is the wholesome lake soup being fouled by waterfowl?

That explanation is somewhat plausible, if the duck's flight from lake to lake is so short that the seeds or eggs do not dry out and become inert and harmless. Anyway, ducks have been migrating for so many millennia that you would think that all the same natural ingredients would already be in every duck-hosting lake.

What about the fish in the lake and the creatures along the shorelines? Don't they all use the soup bowl as toilet bowl? (When I dipped that wine glass into Pelican Lake, remember, I did not then drink out of the glass.)

One shoreline creature polluting the lakes is the lakeside cabin dweller, an irresponsible chef who pours in lawn fertilizer, herbicides, insecticides, and leaches from poorly sited septic tanks. Not to mention indigestible trash.

The current acronym of alarm is *AIS*, aquatic invasive species. Those are plants, invertebrates, fish, or pathogens (disease-causing viruses or bacteria) alien to our lakes, but now infesting them.

No more *ducking* of responsibility! The real culprit for the deterioration of the quality of lake waters due to those aquatic invasive species is—surprise!—the human. It is the invasiveness of the human, not ducks, upon lakes that bears the blame.

Motorboats and trailers are the carriers of the bio-plague. A live well or bilge with soup from one lake is poured and mixed into another lake. The prop of the motor, the axle and wheels of the trailer, and the anchor, bearing life forms from one lake, are dipped into the next lake entered. And so, by boaters the invasives spread.

The process is not only lake-to-lake; it is also ocean-to-ocean, sea-to-shining-sea. The opening of the St. Lawrence Seaway brought worldwide shipping deep into the North American continent, into Lake Superior. Dumped ballast water contained the spiny waterflea, a pest from the Caspian and Black seas, into the Great Lakes, thence by motorboats into inland waters.

The Minnesota lakes' soup now has its international ingredients and seasoning. The Eurasian watermilfoil betrays its origin in its name. (Both Europe and Asia, a bicontinental addition!) Also from across the Atlantic Ocean came the zebra mussel, the fancifully named starry stonewort (an alga), and the Eurasian ruffe (a fish). What next? Oh, there is now a watch out for the New Zealand mudsnail!

Within Pelican Lake the only one of the invasives so far confirmed—(saw it myself)—is the rusty crayfish. (Subject to change without notice.)

Pelican Lake may seem to be a purely local phenomenon and typically Minnesotan. In fact, it is an open receptacle for worldwide influences, very cosmopolitan.

What can be done to restore the health and balance of our lakes by removing the invasives?

Pull them out? Physical removal of invasives is unfeasible or impossible. Poison them out? The invasives have been attacked with lethal chemicals, like copper sulfate and worse, but doesn't that just poison the soup? Put in something to eat them up? An alien predator can be imported to consume the undesirable one, but doesn't that just introduce another problem to be solved? Frustrate their reproduction and spread? A genetic strategy to somehow sterilize the intruders into extinction is being developed; unintended consequences unknown.

Attacking the root and source of the problem, the Minnesota DNR is now recruiting and training volunteers to inspect and decontaminate boats and trailers. Conservation offices are issuing tickets and leveling fines. A public education program is also under way.

Despite all those eradication schemes and preventive efforts, pessimists believe that the problem of aquatic invasive species will never be solved, that the aliens will kill off the natives, as in a horror movie.

Oh, Pelican Lake, what is to become of you?

\* \* \* \* \*

The ecological disaster news this spring and summer (2010) has been the colossal BP oil spill in the Gulf of Mexico. So far unstoppable, the oil gushes from the deep well and spews its filth throughout the Gulf, onto the beaches and marshes of four states, and, farther, eventually into the Atlantic.

The brown pelican of the Southeast, already endangered by toxins and mishaps with fishing nets, may now be coated and smothered with petro-muck to a new extinction threat. Rescuers try to wash the pelicans off, to little avail. Even if the pelican is cleaned, will the bird be set free to become a dipstick?

As I was driving up from Illinois to my cabin for the summer here in northern Minnesota, I was in anxious suspense as to whether our white pelicans of

Pelican Lake would be on their usual summer home. They winter in the Gulf. Had they migrated back north, escaped, before the BP spill in April? Or, exposed to it, were they suffering some hidden harm? Would I find Pelican Lake without any pelicans?

I was relieved and buoyed up when I arrived at my cabin, ran out to the Point, looked across Susan Bay, and saw the white against the blue and the green. Pelicans! Pelicans sailing on the water, pelicans perched on their islets, pelicans in soaring flight and glides.

But what of this coming winter? Leaving the wholesomeness of Pelican Lake, what will the pelicans go back to?

The lakes of the north are directly connected to the Gulf of Mexico, despite the distance and detachment displayed on maps.

\* \* \* \* \*

The town of Orr does not provide trash collection service. Instead, it is up to each resident of the Pelican Lake shoreline community to transport household garbage to a waste transfer station, for which a ticket to dispose must be purchased. Responsibility falls upon the individual.

That is how the Pelican Lake community deals with its trash.

But what about the trash that winds up in Pelican Lake itself? Whose responsibility is that?

I lack the capacity to clean up 11,000 acres of water, but I thought that I might at least take on the

*The Human Presence*

trash collection responsibility for the water of the cove and off the Point—adjacent to my own shoreline property—as well as in Susan Bay.

The litter in Susan Bay is generated by the customers of the resort, transients with no stake in the long-term of Pelican Lake. Most of their trash is aluminum or plastic, which means that if no one picks it up it will be there virtually forever.

To perform my task I transform my canoe into a garbage scow.

I have no scuba outfit for an in-depth effort, so, except for the shallowest water, I am limited to skimming the surface for floating debris. The winds eventually blow the jetsam against the shore; that is where I proceed along my collection route.

I use my eight-foot kayak paddle to draw the litter out of the aquatic vegetation and shoreline brush. I then drop the trash in the bottom of the canoe. Back ashore, I will separate it into the categories of recyclables or garbage for disposal at the transfer station.

To give an idea of what I commonly find and collect, I hereby provide a partial list of the litter removed on one day's recent collection:

- Beer cans (including Hamm's, "From the land of sky-blue waters")
- A whisky bottle thrown onto the shore. (Nature cannot provide her health and healing, if we carry in our poisons with us.)
- Plastic sandwich bags; (sandwiches eaten and digested, empty bags indigestible by the lake)

- A Chicago Cubs cap (from the head of someone who was definitely an alien invasive, that is, a tourist)
- A half-dozen fishing floats, the red-and-white bubble bobbers probably from children's first attempts at fishing
- Plastic tubs, (some bait tubs, the once-occupant worms long-since skewered to death or expired still in the coffin tub, worms then food for worms)
- A rusted insect repellant aerosol can, (the contents of which, if still in the can while in the water, may have leaked out to repel or kill some fish)
- A spent shotgun shell casing, (evidence of a dead duck)
- A truck tire (in the lake? Too massive and heavy to lift into the canoe without capsizing, so I had to leave it.)
- A wire fish basket containing three dead but not yet decayed bluegills, (a failure of someone's knot tying, then, the basket, kept floating by its plastic lid, blown across the lake by an early summer gale)

– – –(One time, my fishing partner and I went into a tackle shop to supply ourselves for an upcoming trip. [A fisherman never has enough or just the right kind of tackle.] As we scanned the hundreds of combinations of sizes and colors of the hundreds of kinds and brands of lures, my partner remarked to me, "Know what? Every single one of these lures we are looking at will wind up at the bottom of some lake or river. Sooner or later." That was a pronounced judgment upon the fisherman's impact upon bodies of water.)– – –

The trash in Pelican Lake is not difficult to find. Aluminum shines in the sun and the bright colors of plastic are conspicuous intrusions into the soft green of boreal Nature. Stirring up the slime and muck during the retrieval is not pleasant, but the odor is organic, anyway.

And so, I discharge my self-imposed duty, rendering my little volunteer service to the community of life in Pelican Lake.

* * * * *

An entertainment feature of this summer's local county fair was The All-American Lumberjack Show.

The show was a competition between two young lumberjacks, a Minnesotan and a Wisconsinite, suitable representatives of the two principal northwoods tree-cutting states. (Was the *All-American* designation meant to exclude the Canadians from the lumberjack fellowship?)

The young men were outfitted with the stereotypical lumberjack plaid shirts, red/black on the one, blue/black on the other. The short sleeves, however, undermined authenticity. Felling trees is not a short-sleeves job.

The exhibition presented a series of tests of lumberjack prowess and skills.

The ringmaster was a senior logger. He explained the events and urged on partisanship in the audience, one side for the red-check shirt, the other side for the blue-.

In the first event, the two competitors had to start their chain-saws, run up an inclined tree trunk, slice off a slab at the tip, race back down, and tag the clipped tip.

The next event was the axe-throw, the target a slice of trunk painted with a bull's-eye on its face and attached to the top of a tripod. The throw was two-handed from behind the head, as the tool was an axe, not a hatchet.

As an intermission from competition, the senior logger demonstrated chain-saw wood sculpting, quickly carving out a small crude chair.

The two young men then returned to compete in quick-cutting slabs of trunk with souped-up high-power chain-saws.

The final event was boom running upon a half-dozen log sections loosely chained end-to-end and floating on a pool of water. The roll of the logs tossed each competitor into the pool with a great splash.

After the competition was completed, each competitor having won a share of the events, woodcarvings were offered for sale.

The lumberjack holds a position in the lore of the north woods similar to that of the cowboy in the West. Paul Bunyan is the Minnesota lumberjack hero. It goes without saying that the romantic adventurous image of the lumberjack has as little to do with contemporary mechanical clear-cut logging as the 19th-century cowboy has to do with modern beef production.

The All-American Lumberjack Show was a nostalgic fantasy; few in the audience could relate to it. The two competitors were real lumberjacks—or, let's say, loggers—, but their high-power chain-saws instead of muscle-powered saw blades distanced them from the rough manual labor of the traditional way.

Significantly, the senior logger ringmaster introduced them not in terms of how many years of working or how many acres cut, but in terms of how many awards each man had earned in lumberjack shows. In other words, they were not primarily loggers; they were entertainers. Their work was just for show.

I presume they earned their living and were paid per performance, not per board foot of timber felled. In the off-season of the show circuit, they probably drove some huge machine to down and move timber.

The other Minnesota exploitive economic enterprise, mining, is not so easily romanticized. There is nothing glamorous about digging and tunneling, which are necessarily associated with burrowing mammals with dirty claws. What Minnesota promotes about mining is its essential economic value, not its way of life. Also, iron lacks the get-rich-quick allure of gold.

Most of the centuries-old trees of the northern virgin forest long gone, today's logging is for pulpwood, which means clear-cutting, stripping entire hillsides down to bare rock. One such scalped slope disfigures a ridge behind the south shore high above Pelican Lake.

The usual logging practice is to leave a narrow strip of woods along lakeshores, so that the tourists in boats remain under the illusion that they are surrounded by forest on all sides, when, in actuality, behind the curtain of trees are down-to-rock clear-cut tracts. In that presentation, the concealing curtain is the show.

\* \* \* \* \*

Another northwoods entertainment, unexpected because so seemingly out-of-place, is the rodeo. Yet the North Star Stampede has been held annually for more than 60 years on a ranch just outside Effie, Minnesota.

This north woods is the wild. A rodeo is a pageant of taming.

All the animals that surrounded the bands of primitive early humans were wild. But the human, that cunning animal, gradually perceived that some wild animals could be made serviceable. So the humans captured, tamed, and made serviceable:—Wild canines into protecting watchdogs and hunting helpers, wild felines into mousers, wild grazers into livestock, wild fowl into poultry, and, much later, wild equines into horses for labor and conveyance.

Animals resistant to taming, and so useless, were killed or driven off to be kept at a distant remove from the humans and their acquired functional menagerie.

And so the earth was divided into two realms: The first, still as God created it, the all-wild natural world. The second, as the human assembled it, the enclaves of human society with its economy of confined, tethered, and penned animals. That economy provided hides for clothing as well as meat, milk, and eggs for food, resources at-hand and reproducible for future need.

## The Human Presence

When I arrived just before the opening of the North Star Stampede, I was impressed by the sheer number of horses on the grounds, as if all the horses of Minnesota were arrived there. But no herd of free wild mustangs, those. Each horse had a rider who controlled and directed the horse through its paces in rehearsal for its role in the show.

The rodeo exhibition itself consisted of a variety of attempts to subdue and tame: Steer wrestling and bull riding, calf roping and team roping, bronco riding—both bareback and saddled—, and, as a demonstration of exacting horsemanship, the fast obstacle course of barrel racing.

Just as the lumberjack show was a demonstration of prowess in logging skills, so the rodeo was a showoff of what the cowboy can do. In both cases, cooperative work becomes competitive play.

From the lumberjack show, we infer that this human society lives in shelters of wood; from the rodeo that these people are beef eaters.

The grandstand was packed and the audience enthusiastic. Even so, as at the lumberjack show, I detected a lack of relatedness between the spectators and the spectacle. The close connectedness of people to animals, as on a farm or ranch, is an experience alien to urbanites and suburbanites, the vast majority of our current population. Keeping a household pet is a pitiful reminiscence of that relatedness.

Animal life no longer attracts us much. We are more fascinated by our connections to the electronic devices of our own devising, the inert contrivances for human social relatedness, our work and our diversion.

We have become creatures of the technosphere, almost wholly detached from organic Nature.

The very urban town I recently moved to passed an ordinance prohibiting animal shows within the city. That ordinance was aimed at circuses and rodeos. The grounds of the ordinance was an objection to *cruelty to animals*. (I presume the ordinance was so worded as to permit dog shows.) The ordinance was an empty after-the-fact, for the great Ringling Brothers Circus was folding its tent for the last time; nor had any rodeo ever threatened to come to our town.

As for *cruelty to animals*: Yes, the rodeo animals were subjected to roughhousing, but the main cruelty perpetrated seemed that upon the rodeo cowboys. They were thrown, stepped on, kicked, crushed, and otherwise beaten up by the heavyweights they grappled with. Paramedics rushed in when one cowboy did not get up after his bronco fell on him. (Whether first-aid service was available to the animals I did not determine.)

Why rodeo cowboys choose the abuse is a wonder to me. Most of them wind up all crippled. (As for the rodeo cattle, they may wind up as some city dweller's dinner, this a beef-eating society, as I inferred before.)

The rodeo, like the circus, exults in our taming of the wild animals. What, are we now feeling some scruple, some guilt, for our exploitation of animals, that we now turn away from exhibitions of that triumphalism?

\* \* \* \* \*

I saw a sign that read "Jack Pine Ridge Forest Management Road." I drove in to find out what "Forest Management" might mean there.

The gravel road led me to a clear-cut hillside. That is what "Forest Management" signified. Jack Pine Ridge has had its jack pines removed.

A forest bulldozed. The scene was one of desolation, as if after some massive natural catastrophe or unremitting attack of total warfare.

The road wound around and ended at a huge sandpit and sand pile, an excavation and heaping-up of barrenness.

I got out of the car and ascended the hill toward the ridge.

Jack pines had been there, all right. The hillside was littered with their carcasses and dismembered body parts,—trunks, limbs, branches, and twigs. There was so much waste in the clear-cutting. Were all those left-behind jack pine trunks already dead, rotten, and useless when the loggers arrived to their task?

The ridge must have been logged a while ago, for the hillside was overgrown with raspberries, wildflowers, some coarse grasses, and other pioneers in the colonization of bare rocky land.

Beneath the new ground cover I saw many jack pine cones,—the promise and hope of a new jack pine forest to come. Perhaps the forest managers will torch the hillside to provoke the opening of the jack pine cones.

I climbed over the debris to the very top of the ridge. From that lofty standpoint I beheld a sweeping panorama of the Minnesota woodlands.

*Woodlands.* I wondered about the meaning of that word. Does it describe the land of the life of the woods, or does it denote merely the source location of an inert commodity, wood? I take it at the former meaning.

No other clear-cut gashes in the panorama, fortunately.

What an awe-inspiring expanse! A view no tourist is likely to see, for the place is not on the list of the state's promoted itineraries. Loggers have looked upon this view, but they likely saw it in terms of more work to do, more money to be made. Jack pines and the other trees of the Minnesota forests are inedible, but they are the medium of exchange for the food on the loggers' family table.

Behind me, below the ridge, was a dense stand of living jack pines. The loggers' license must have stopped short of them. So, they remain uncut, at least until a new survey and a new license to clear-cut.

On the denuded hillside I could find no jack pine sprouts from the cones. There was one lone tree still standing in the center of the ridge, a slender red pine. For some reason, the loggers didn't want it, didn't take it. Odd one out, that red pine now has the entire hillside all to itself. No more competition for sunlight from the jack pines; humans intervened in that competition. The clear-cutting provided an opportunity for growth, but also a vulnerability. That pine has no fellows to help shield it from destructive winds.

As for any wildlife on the stripped hillside, I saw only a solitary raven. The raven was flying up the hillside toward the ridge, but, spying me so conspicuous below, she changed course, flew behind the cover of the remaining jack pines, around and far from me, then off again. A funereal figure, a haunting spook whose harsh croak upon departure served as epitaph upon the dead-and-gone of Jack Pine Ridge.

\* \* \* \* \*

Several summers of drought, some late-winter ice storms, and the *derecho* of July, 2012 have taken a heavy toll of the trees on the peninsula to the Point. The *derecho* was especially destructive, breaking or uprooting the tall pines, which fell upon and levelled the spindly birches and smaller balsams. The consequence is a forestscape of prostrate trunks, broken branches, and a litter thicket of jumbled brush, boughs, and sticks. In all, a demoralizing scene of wreckage.

Since the *derecho*, I have done some cleanup, but the ruin was so extensive as to be daunting to an aging woodsman.

I arrived this summer (2014) to find the great white pine outside the cabin bedroom completely dead. I was not surprised, because, last summer when I saw that only a few branches bore green needles, I enquired to get a reference to a local logger who would execute the inevitable.

When I now gazed upward and saw my neighbor eagle on his usual perch on the barren branch atop the corpse of the pine, he appeared to me not as eagle, but as vulture awaiting consumption of the dead.

Life had gone out of the great pine, but it still stood amidst the continuing life of the forest. It would produce no more cones for the red squirrel, but it might remain standing long enough to provide nest holes for woodpecker or flicker and perhaps a lodging for some mammal in the base of its trunk. It would still host lichens and mosses, as well as serve as food for insects and the microbial agents of decomposition. Yes, even a dead tree is useful for the furtherance of life.

Never mind all that, my main consideration was that a storm from the south might put the pine in bed with me while slicing my cabin in half. Having gone through the personal experience of *derecho* and desiring nights of sound sleep without apprehension, I decided that the tree must come down as soon as possible.

So, I would follow the general human pattern of relationship to Nature and the environment, that is, what was not wanted would be removed. I was innocent of exploitation, true. I was not about to kill natural life for my personal economic benefit, but I would be interfering with and pre-empting the natural process of gradual recycling of the dead into new life. No matter. The great pine had to come down.

The logger arrived to take on the task of felling singlehandedly. He would not climb the tree to cut it down in sections, he told me; too dangerous. He would fell the tree entire. It's the tree that should be felled, not the feller.

The path for the fall had already been opened up by the *derecho*, so no living trees would be much affected. A red pine, almost as massive as the great white pine, was downed along the desired direction. The logger started up his chain-saw and sliced that one up, nipping off the stubs, so that the trunk would lay flat and not cause a kickback of the tree coming down.

That completed and the path of proposed fall clear, the logger then cut out a notch from the side of the great pine facing away from the cabin. That knee-high opening would serve as a hinge to tip the tree. The logger said that the tree stood close to the vertical, so there should be no problem directing its fall.

He then notched the tree again at knee-height, now on the cabin side of the tree. He pounded a hard plastic wedge into that cut. Slipping the chain-saw blade into the cut in advance of the wedge, he sliced a bit more through the trunk. He then pounded the wedge in farther.

He alternated slicing and pounding in the wedge, until the wedge was fully within the trunk and the tree had taken on a pronounced lean toward the open path. The base of the trunk creaked with the strain of the shifted weight of the entire tree.

At each stage of the process, the logger looked upward to check the direction of the lean. He proceeded carefully and methodically.

At last, he sliced through. The great pine fell straight down in a piece, except for its highest branches, which shattered on impact.

The logger then chain-sawed through the entire length of the prostrate trunk at intervals of 16", the length suitable after splitting for use in a wood burning furnace. A winter warming resource was now at hand, although I'm a summer resident only and the neighbors all seem to have already converted their *derecho* casualties into a fuel store for several winters.

The cylinders of the trunk, now lying in a line, looked like a stack of checkers that had tumbled over from Paul Bunyan's checker game.

The logger finished up by reducing some deadfalls, limbs, and branches to manageable length for hauling away.

Janet and I then had him in for coffee. In leisurely conversation, he proved to be an easy-going and personable Scandinavian Minnesotan.

A few days later, I conducted an arboreal autopsy of the great pine. I first examined the still-rooted stump. The base of the tree had rotted through the heartwood. I pulled up staves and brittle splinters of what had been the core of support for the tree.

Proceeding along the row of sliced sections, I found more heartwood decay, which tapered off gradually. Some higher sections were solid all through, then there was decay again. Crumbling the rotted wood in my hand, I came across a large white grub and black carpenter ants. The heartwood of one section had been reduced to a wet reddish-brown mush.

I wanted to get at the age of the tree, so I turned one sound disc section flat. The annual growth rings from the drought years were so slim as to be indistinct, even under the magnifying glass. Also, the crude cutting of the chain-saw had abraded the exposed surface. Brushing the surface smooth and pouring on some water to darken and swell the wood, I was able to make out at least 169 years of life.

The great white pine is no more. And the evicted eagle has taken a new outlook perch on a dying pine on Hahne island.

Afternoon sunlight now enters the bedroom of my cabin. Through the window there is a new glimpse of Pelican Lake all the way to its south shore. The seclusion I have felt when looking through that window has been lost. But now there is sunlight and an opening for the emergence of new arboreal life.

\* \* \* \* \*

One month after I spent the day observing the loon family and writing the section about them, I was on the Point when the two young ones, chicks no longer, came paddling by side-by-side. Their parents not near, they advanced into the wind with a confident new independence.

A motorboat came on speeding toward them. The young loons now floated on the direct line between that boat and the resort pier.

The motorboat roared upon the young loons. They dove in an attempt to escape, but the boat ran right over the top of them, then roared on to the resort.

I looked out in alarm, as the series of waves rolled away from the scene.

"Come back up! Come up!" I cried out to the loons, as I panned searching back-and-forth over the surface.

I watched and watched, but the young loons did not come back up. They had been pulled under the boat and drowned. The boat prop may have shredded them into a slurry of feathers and flesh and bones.

A while later, the mother loon came to the area where she had left her young ones. She called, but they were no longer there to come.

*****

An old lady provides three bird feeders for her "feathered friends". Of course the birds spill a lot of seeds, so the lady also enjoys a companionship with the chipmunks and the red squirrels drawn to a feeding.

Meanwhile, the man who is her next-door cabin neighbor has become bothered by the chipmunks and squirrels invading his shed or gnawing away at the wooden doors and windows of his cabin. He has a pellet rifle at his front door. Whenever a chipmunk or squirrel comes by—perhaps on the way to the lady's bird feeders—, he opens the door, takes up his rifle, and kills it.

So the human attitude toward, and treatment of, the creatures of the woods:—On the one hand, nurturance of what is regarded as outside pets; on the other hand, extermination of what is regarded as intrusive pests.

*****

I took a stroll down the short gravel road that provides access to my cabin. The road edges the woods on the curve of the small cove east of the Point.

My purpose was to admire the fairyland of ferns in the shade along the road and down in the lowland.

A young man, a guest of the resort, approached from the other side of the road, as I caressed the feathery fronds of a fern.

"There's a deer just up ahead of you," he said to me.

"She had triplets last year," I informed him.

I proceeded slowly forward, the young man, I could sense, following along in the grassy clearing cut by the resort owners on their side of the road.

The doe came into view, standing by the trunk of a fallen birch tree.

"If I had my bow, that deer would be dead right now!" the young man exclaimed in a tone of deep longing.

The doe stood in a peculiar stance, her rump toward us, her head twisted over her back to look at us. She appeared to have no forelegs or chest.

"Sarah, Sarah, bring me the camera!" the young man cried out.

I stood still, gazing at the doe, she equally still, gazing at me.

In a minute, I felt the young man creeping closer behind me. I then heard the click of the camera shutter.

The doe stared at the two of us with fixed attention, but without expression or emotion.

That black nose, round open eyes, erect ears.

"She has a beautiful color this time of year," the young man said.

At last, the doe stepped over the birch trunk and, after a few tiptoes, disappeared into the brush.

I continued a bit farther on the road, leaving the young man behind.

Then I descended from the road fully into the fairyland of ferns.

\* \* \* \* \*

A local man decided to hunt some rabbits. He took up his rifle, loaded it, and headed out.

He walked onto a nearby Forest Service dirt road wending into the woods.

He hadn't gone very far when he saw a red fox trotting on the other side of the road up ahead.

The fox detected the man's presence, stopped, and looked back.

It did not then run off into the woods or slink away into the underbrush, as the man expected it to do. Instead, the fox turned around and stood facing the approaching man.

The man and the fox were now directly across from each other.

The fox gazed steadily at the man, not tense or menacing, just looking, looking at him.

The man was puzzled by the fox's behavior.

Then, remembering that he was hunting, he clutched at the rifle in his hands.

The fox now sat down, relaxed and comfortable with meeting a man.

The hunter raised his rifle. The fox sitting so still, the shot could be easy and accurate. The hunter aimed and fired, the bullet right through the eye of the fox.

The bullet then penetrating the brain, there was no death struggle, not even a twitch. The fox just collapsed into a small heap of fur and gangly limbs. One moment he was alive. The next moment he was dead.

The hunter continued along the road but did not see any rabbits that day.

A week later, he happened to be in conversation with a neighbor woman. She mentioned that, as she and her husband were having breakfast every day, they would see through the cabin window a red fox hanging around. It was a handsome fellow, but scrawny, she said. So she decided to put out some meat scraps and see whether the fox would take them.

As she came out to lay down the pan of food, the fox withdrew slightly, to the edge of the woods. The woman returned to breakfast with her husband, the two of them watching through the window. After some while the fox timidly approached the pan of food, gulped it down, and ran off.

Each day thereafter, she said, she would put out the food and the fox would come to eat it. One day the fox was even there before her, sitting and waiting for her to bring the food.

But then, she said, the fox didn't come anymore. She continued to put the food out, but the fox didn't come. It was only crows that arrived to clean up the scraps. And so she stopped putting out any food.

While the man was telling me the story, I sensed no regret, shame, or even awareness of irony. He reported in a straight-forward, matter-of-fact way, not interjecting any comments, either during or after. He just told me the story, for me to make of it what I would.

* * * * *

A neighbor told me that a dog on a leash in a backyard was attacked and killed by wolves.

The dog owner did what anyone would do in such a situation. He called the federal government.

The government has taken on the responsibility of *managing* wolves. Wolves used to be exterminated as vermin (or is it *varmints*?). Now, in our more enlightened time, concerned as we are about the welfare of *threatened* and *endangered species*, we manage wolves and the problems they present.

The federal agents responded to the dog owner's complaint by shooting, trapping, and otherwise exterminating the six wolves that had killed the dog.

To my mind, a dog on a leash is not worth six wild wolves.

"Those wolves were mangy," my neighbor said. "That was why they couldn't hunt and catch anything but a dog on a leash."

His use of the word "mangy" I took as further justification for the killing of the wolves; it was almost a mercy killing.

My neighbor went on to tell of another local, one who has cattle, which he protects by shooting any wolf that shows up anywhere near the pasture. Apparently, if you want to hunt wolves, buy yourself a cow. Even in northern Minnesota, where it is the cow, not the wolf, that is the intruder.

"This is not to get out..." my neighbor then said, "but...." He then told me of a local who hunts and kills wolves for no reason and without any consultation with, or approval from, the federal government wildlife management service.

Humans against wolves, one of the most relentless campaigns of interspecies warfare.

The wolf has nothing to say against humans, but we have had plenty to say in the war propaganda against the wolf.

The wolf, we argue in indictment, is *cunning*.

How cunning? Do we mean cunning like the hunter who dons camouflage clothing, douses himself in a chemical to mask his natural scent, and takes to the woods with a fire-spewing steel mechanism that can kill at two hundred yards? He has already been setting out corn as bait or a salt block to lure mineral-craving deer to the area. Perhaps he has also set out a trail camera to monitor the deer's movements.

Or cunning like the one in a constructed natural looking vegetative well-named *blind* blowing on a clever device that sounds to a duck so like a duck? He has previously set out dozens of decoys, even mechanical ones, that look to a high flyer just like a flock of his fellows.

Or cunning like the bow hunter dressed in clothing patterned in bark-and-leaves perched in wait in a tree stand placed high up, because he knows that wary deer look around for danger, but can't conceive any danger from above?

What about wolf cunning? It's a sniffing about and a chasing after.

The wolf is *cruel, vicious, a bloodthirsty killer*, we press our case with a moral judgment.

Yes, carnivores kill to eat, a matter of the course of necessity. But *cruel*?

So cruel as to slaughter any and every kind of animal that can be mummified and set up as a cadaverous ornament of the house? Kill a moose and chop off its head to hang on the wall? Scalp and flay any furbearer for a rug to step upon and warm bare feet? Kill a bear to take its testicles as trophy? (I saw that myself.) Poison, trap, maim, persecute, extirpate any other animal whose presence may be merely a nuisance?

As for *bloodthirsty*, what about the *pow!-pow!-pow!* blasting of duck after duck after duck, until the dog is too winded to go swimming for all the floating corpses? Or the deer hunter who hangs the slain deer from its hind legs in a tree, slits its belly from anus to throat and eviscerates? Plenty of blood in that procedure, whether or not the blood is actually drunk.

Oh, I forgot *vicious*. Invidious comparisons present themselves there, too.

Predators do not tolerate the presence and competition of other predators. Coyotes will kill foxes, and wolves will kill coyotes. And we humans will kill wolves, even though any question of competition has long been decided.

\* \* \* \* \*

Last night, I was invited to a social gathering of local cabin residents for some sweets and conversation.

I was the only solo there. The other participants were six married couples, strangers to me except for the hosting couple, distant kin of my wife.

The women all gathered around a table in the screen house for their chitchat. The husbands and I sat on the open deck to engage in man-talk.

The men all in late middle-age, it was not surprising that the conversation opened with health issues and medical matters,—treatments for skin cancers, prostate problems, and such.

A few anecdotes about local characters were told and laughed over. The men inquired of one another about mutual acquaintances not seen for a while and absent from the gathering.

Then, as we were all in the midst of a woods-and-waters environment, the conversation turned to wildlife. An eagle alighting on a nearby tree drew our attention and was the stimulus to the talk.

First, we heard from one who had seen the mountain lion. I remarked that he should try to get a photo of it, as its proven presence in Minnesota would certainly be newsworthy.

After I mentioned that I had just been to the bear sanctuary, the subject of the general conversation turned to bears. What to do if confronted by an aggressive bear.

One man, whose son lived in Alaska, told of someone there who used to carry a pistol on his walks with his dog. On one of those walks, the dog, which had gone on ahead, suddenly ran back to his master in a panic, followed by a charging grizzly bear. The man drew his handgun, fired three shots that missed, then three shots that struck the bear, killing it virtually at the feet of the shooter.

The theme of animal killing was then passed around the assemblage.

Another man, who had been a farmer, told how he had discovered chewed ears of his growing sweet corn.

Thinking it was raccoons, he went to the store and bought a poison he called *fly bait*. He poured a can of Coca-Cola into a shallow pan, stirred in the fly bait granules and set the pan in the cornfield. The next day he found the corpses...of skunks.

The group laughed at that one.

To prove that he could kill off raccoons, the ex-farmer then told of the time that a raccoon had invaded the loft of his tool shed. He set out the fly bait and Coca-Cola cocktail once again, killed the raccoon...and all four of her kits.

He also used to enjoy shooting gophers from the tractor, when he was a teenager. He was in competition on the body count with his brother on another tractor. The fun and sport lasted until one day, when the tractor hit a bump, the pistol went off accidentally and the bullet went through the tractor's distributor cap.

That story led into the topic of hunting weapons.

The man sitting opposite me was a bow hunter, both longbow and crossbow. He discussed his equipment and told how an arrow of his went clean through the deer and half buried itself in the ground. A listener asked him how far the deer ran before it fell down and died.

The bow hunter and the man next to me then began to talk about firearms, their properties and capabilities. Both men discovered that they had in common the enjoyment of watching military programs on cable TV.

One military incident related on a program was from the Vietnam War. An American sniper had snuck into range of a Viet Cong officer's tent. The sniper observed the officer's daily routine, then, one early morning as the officer had just emerged from the tent and stretched out his arms to the new day, the sniper shot him full in the chest.

The next incident was from our current war in Afghanistan. A half-dozen U.S. soldiers in urban combat were surrounded by Taliban. The soldiers radioed for help. Helicopters were brought in to drop snipers on distant rooftops. The snipers shot three of the Taliban besiegers, all in the head. The snipers hidden and so far away, the Taliban still alive could not tell where the fire that had killed their comrades had come from. They backed away to a wider perimeter, where the American snipers with their long-range weapons shot a few more in the head. Further retreat kept widening the perimeter, until the few surviving Taliban scattered and fled.

Then there was talk of rifles that could shoot around corners and bullets with a programmed flight that went around obstacles to the kill and the most deadly types of ammunition, calibers, penetrating power, and on and on.

At last, darkness having arrived, along with sprinkles of rain onto the open deck, the party broke up.

I returned to my cabin oppressed by a deep disquiet.

\* \* \* \* \*

## The Human Presence

Nature scatters life, fills with life.

Scatters spores, seeds, eggs, and the offspring of live-bearing creatures. The generation of life is a process of infinite variety of kinds and superabundance of individuals. A scattershot process of effusive fecundity.

The prolific random scattering is to the effect of a filling-up of the entire earth with living organisms. Nature would produce life cheek-to-cheek, if it weren't for the restrictive factors of environment and the competition of all species and individuals for limited resources. The whole earth, as every distinct ecosystem within it, has a *carrying capacity*. Then too, the hard facts of landscape (or water chemistry) and climate may exclude certain kinds of life by being outside a tolerable range or lacking some life requirements.

Even so, if a tree cannot grow in a particular place, Nature will grow a shrub; if not enough rain to sustain a shrub, then grass; if no soil for grass, why, then, lichens and moss on a rock.

The vegetation in these north woods tends to be dense, trees tight together, each struggling upward for its share of sun. Meanwhile, the shade-tolerant trees, nothing deterred by light deprivation, make a go-of-it underneath. Below them the shrubs, wildflowers, weeds, herbs, grasses, mosses, and such. Life will layer on unto fill-fullment.

Nourished by rooted vegetative life, profuse populations of bacteria, insects, birds, and mammals animate the woods. Some life-form or other occupies every conceivable niche. Despite the check of a cold-winter northern climate, the liveliness of life permeates this environment. Nature has scattered and filled to the limits of possibility.

The human culls and empties.

Nature's profusion presents an obstacle to the human's designs. The only human interest is the self-interest. In order for man to take the place all for himself, other life must be displaced.

Most human action against Nature and life has been a culling-out of the humanly unusable and a nurturing promotion of the for-us-only. That's agriculture and husbandry, functional land, functional animals. What the human can't exploit doesn't deserve to exist.

The human kills off, eradicates, pushes into extinc- tion. Little by little, the human is emptying the environment of its manifold forms of life.

The human is pushing Nature into impoverishment, depleting all that is natural, both wild animals and life-supporting environments.

For, it is not only trees that are clear-cut; it is entire environments. (Blessed are the barren wastes, immune to the exploitive rapacity of the human!)

Ultimately, the human will empty out Nature herself. In the inventory of the earth, life-forms are being replaced by inert contrivances. The biosphere will be fully transformed into a technosphere.

## Postscript

Friend, fellow *voyageur*, why is it that we no longer travel together?

We had some great experiences, you and I. We paddled over many waters, portaged through many passageways between lakes. You and I, in the same canoe. You and I, sharing the burdens in the carry-over of the portage. You and I, sleeping side-by-side in the same tent, sharing the same meal, communicating one with the other in the midst of the silence of the wilderness.

And now, you no longer seek me out to share your experiences, to travel together in the same canoe.

Why have you forgotten me? Why have I become of no more interest to you? Why can we no longer share the course of the voyage through life?

Friend, fellow *voyageur*, why, why is it that we no longer travel together?

(end)

Made in the USA
Lexington, KY
30 November 2019